BIPOLAR BATTLE PLAN WORKBOOK

Troy Steven

BATTLE PRESS
FOUNDED 2020

Battle Press

SATELLITE BEACH, FLORIDA

Bipolar Battle Plan Workbook

ISBN: 979-8-9957990-5-4 (SC)
ISBN: 979-8-9957990-6-1 (Ebook)

Printed in the United States of America.

First edition.

Additional Books by Troy Steven:

BREAKING BIPOLAR: BREAK THE HOLD BIPOLAR DISORDER HAS OVER YOUR LIFE

AFTER YOUR BIPOLAR DISORDER: BIPOLAR HEAL THYSELF

BIPOLAR OMENS: TRUE STORIES OF A BIPOLAR TRAVELER

Docudrama:

BREAKING BIPOLAR (Coming in 2027)

CONTENTS

Thanks

First and foremost, I must thank John, Ruth, Gary, Scott, and Jane who graciously agreed to be interviewed about their experiences and struggles with bipolar disorder. Their advice, stories, and wisdom are included throughout the pages of this book, illuminating the reality of being bipolar.

I would also like to express my gratitude to the many people who have seen me through the writing of this workbook by providing support, exploring ideas, offering constructive comments, and assisting in the editing and proofreading process.

DISCLAIMER

Dedication

This book is dedicated to the Bipolar Warriors who, despite being bipolar, carved their way to greatness.

Also, to my kids Jennifer, Rachel, Jeremy, and Natalie, and grandchildren Braelynn, Karmella, Moses and Claire who are a constant source of inspiration.

Foreword

It is my pleasure to write this Foreword. I find this workbook educational for patients who are newly diagnosed, or have been coping with bipolar disorder for years, and wanting to change the course of their life. This book is well organized in a concise style outlining how to better understand and avoid the road to destruction. I cannot emphasize enough the need to understand what is happening to you or a loved one.

This workbook gives you suggestions on how to find a psychiatrist and work with them. There are many good concepts on learning how to give feedback on your medications and the danger of stopping taking them and ending up back to square one. Talk Therapy will help you to learn positive ways to think, process your feelings and learn to live a better life. Troy talks of the benefits of online and DBSA support groups for peer support. Learn about mood diaries and good books that may also help. You'll need to become your own best advocate.

This is a well thought out endeavor by this author, who has battled bipolar disorder for over 25 years. Having gone the long road Troy wants to help others avoid the pitfalls he had to endure.

Dr. Beth Ann Mahoney, DO

Preface

This workbook is an enhancement of my book, Breaking Bipolar, with worksheets, checklists, tools and additional subject matter to help you win the war against Bipolar Disorder.

I wrote this workbook with the intent of helping those who are suffering from bipolar disorder, as well as to help myself. Bipolar disorder is a condition that cannot be ignored or underestimated. The implications are simply too serious: such as suicide, or living a crippled, limited life, reckless or violent behavior, financial problems, personal and professional relationships undermined, loss of self-respect, and sometimes the most tragic, giving up on your dreams.

Millions suffer daily; struggling alone, oftentimes afraid to confess to others or confront their condition, too many go unnoticed and untreated until it's too late.

Unfortunately, I must include myself in this list. I am bipolar, having struggled since 1993 and I am all too aware of what it takes to confront and battle this illness. I have survived three major episodes, which have resulted in three separate visits to psychiatric hospitals, one due to a suicide attempt. Despite the cost of these episodes, I maintained a career in engineering, obtained a master's degree, published 75 books for other authors and currently work as an aerospace engineer. I am also the proud parent of four awesome kids and blessed with four grandchildren. This goes far beyond me, though.

The idea of creating a bipolar battle plan began after I attempted suicide in 2007. I almost succeeded. Afterward, I promised myself I would do anything and everything I could to keep it from happening again. I realized I had to make major changes in the way I was managing the illness, in my treatment plan, and in the way I was living my life.

With hopes to help others, I have had to confront my darkest thoughts and demons in order to write this book, which has not been easy. I had to face the root cause of attempting to take my life. Today I have found balance and achieved security by creating a battle plan to overcome bipolar illness. I have successfully used the plan over time to remain episode free and advance toward achieving my dreams.

Everyone is different, but this disorder and how it affects us is predominantly consistent. We experience ups and downs sometimes so severe that feeling utterly average would be welcome. Good days, waking without that uninvited guest lurking, waiting to pounce–sometimes seem so rare. It is a struggle to gain the trust and respect of others, but most of all, to trust that things will get better, that this episode will pass, yet there will be another battle in the future. There are no quick fixes. It helps to accept that this is a lifelong struggle requiring immediate attention and long-term remedies.

The workbook you are holding in your hands promises one thing: to provide you with the weapons and training to fight bipolar illness strategically, intelligently, and as a warrior. Equipped with a battle plan to combat bipolar disorder you will be well-armed to achieve victory. This is your life – you don't get another!

Note:

Five people with bipolar disorder agreed to be interviewed for this workbook about their experiences and struggles with bipolar disorder. Their advice, stories, and wisdom are included throughout illuminating the reality of being bipolar.

Introduction

I want to thank you for your bravery in taking charge of your battle. The purpose is to provide you with the knowledge, skills and battle plan tools to win the war against bipolar disorder.

"Victory means living a productive, happy life—and making your dreams come true!"

For those of us who are bipolar, it is important to understand that we are facing a highly complex situation, and we can't hope to change it until we arm ourselves with the necessary psychological and intellectual capacity.

To effectively battle bipolar disorder, the best solution is to follow a lifelong battle plan (also known as a whole-life wellness plan) based upon the expert recommendations of the medical community. The consensus is that successful treatment of bipolar disorder depends on diligently following a comprehensive treatment plan including medication, continuous education regarding the illness, communication with your psychiatrist and therapist, having a strong support system and helping yourself by making healthy lifestyle choices. This workbook gives you that plan.

The Bipolar Battle Plan consists of nine weapons. Each weapon has a dedicated chapter with accompanying checklists and worksheets. There is room to journal your thoughts at the end of each chapter.

The nine weapons in the Bipolar Battle Plan are outlined below:

1. **Make a Contingency Plan (Weapon 1)**

The purpose of the contingency plan is to keep you alive, out of the hospital, and out of jail when you are having a bipolar episode. It is the last line of defense to keep a manic episode from skyrocketing out of control or a depressive episode from plummeting to disaster. Included in this chapter is a form to put your contingency plan in writing.

2. **Enemy Recon – Understanding Bipolar Disorder (Weapon 2)**

- What is bipolar disorder?
- Bipolar disorder is a biological illness
- Five types of bipolar disorder
- Mania early warning signs
- Common symptoms of mania
- Common symptoms of hypomania
- Depression early warning signs
- Common symptoms of depression
- Bipolar disorder triggers
- Sleep disturbances
- Causes of bipolar disorder

3. **Optimize Your Medication (Weapon 3)**

- The role of medication in treating bipolar disorder
- Bipolar heal thyself
- Getting the most out of bipolar medications
- Researching your medications
- Becoming your own mental detector
- Rating your medications
- The perfect medication cocktail
- Beware of side effects

4. **Find the Right Psychiatrist (Weapon 4)**

- How to rate a psychiatrist
- Typical questions to ask a psychiatrist
- Typical questions a psychiatrist may ask
- How to get the most out of appointments with your psychiatrist

- When to consider getting a new psychiatrist
- Pointers on how to find a new psychiatrist

5. Train Your Mind (Weapon 5)

- The path with heart
- Self-importance is your greatest enemy
- Stop the internal dialogue
- Positive and negative emotions
- Process of autosuggestion
- Death is stalking you
- Stalk yourself
- Face fear head on
- Running the bipolar marathon

6. Train Your Body (Weapon 6)

- Healthy habits
- It is crucial to get enough sleep
- Stay away from sick people at all costs
- Stay hydrated
- Eat healthy
- Exercise
- Make Love
- Get fresh air and sunshine
- Drugs and alcohol

7. Recovering from a Bipolar Episode (Weapon 7)

- Physical symptoms of stress
- Practice relaxation
- Promote positive thinking
- Use coping techniques
- Ways therapy can help
- Things people do that do not aid in your recovery

8. What you need to know about Psychiatric Hospitals (Weapon 8)

- Voluntary Check in
- Involuntary commitment
- Reasons to check into a psychiatric hospital
- Go with the flow
- Contacting your employer
- How hospitalization can help
- Don't leave the hospital too soon

9. Legal Rights (Weapon 9)

- Legal rights as an employee
- The American with Disabilities Act
- The laws governing involuntary commitment
- Legal rights as a patient in a psychiatric hospital
- Legal rights regarding medicine refusal
- The benefit of having a Psychiatric Advance Directive (PAD)
- Your legal rights for getting discharged from a Psychiatric hospital

Resources:

Always remember there are help lines with people on call at all times. Some examples include:

- National Suicide Prevention Lifeline (1-800-273-8255)
- Mental Health Hot Line (1-844-549-4266)
- Substance Abuse and Mental Health Helpline (1-800-662-4357)
- Crisis Text Line (Text 'HOME' to 741741)
- Most importantly, if you are in trouble and your life is on the line, dial 911.

Most of you have a cell phone, tablet, or computer. There are a number of available Apps for battling bipolar disorder that you may find to be helpful.

Bipolar Disorder Apps: 10 Best for Daily Support

https://threewindows.com/bipolar-disorder-apps/#1_eMoods_Bipolar_Mood_Tracker

Top 7 Mood-Tracking Apps for Bipolar Disorder

https://www.bphope.com/bipolar-buzz/bipolar-lifestyle-top-6-apps-to-track-your-moods/

Depression Bipolar Support Alliance (DBSA)

DBSA offers wellness tips, education, and peer support for people living with depression and bipolar disorder.

https://www.dbsalliance.org/support/

DBSA Wellness Wheel – See Appendix A

https://www.dbsalliance.org/wellness/wellness-toolbox/dbsa-wellness-wheel/

National Alliance on Mental Illness (NAMI)

NAMI is the nation's largest mental health organization, providing support, education and advocacy for people affected by mental illness.

https://www.nami.org/

Notes

Bipolar Questionnaire

Answer the following questions to determine your current state of mind and overall understanding of bipolar disorder. There are no right or wrong answers. Jot down anything that comes to mind while answering the questions. To gauge your understanding, after completing the workbook return and answer the questions again.

1. Do you feel manic?

2. Do you feel depressed?

3. Is your mood cycling from highs to lows?

4. Do you feel anxious?

5. Are you angry or irritable?

6. Do you feel hopeless?

7. Do you feel suicidal?

8. Do you have reasons to live? What are the top 3 reasons?

9. Do you feel withdrawn from friends or family?

10. Do you feel trapped – like there's no way out?

11. Do you feel dangerous to yourself or others?

12. Do you have someone to talk to about how you are feeling? What is their name or names?

13. Are you using drugs and/or alcohol?

14. Have you been getting good sleep?

15. Have you been taking your medications regularly and at the same time every day?

16. Have you stopped taking your medications?

17. Are you having any side effects due to the medication? What are they?

18. Have you been getting sunshine?

19. Have you been drinking lots of fluids?

20. Have you been eating healthy?

21. Are you knowledgeable about bipolar disorder?

22. Do you see a psychiatrist and/or therapist?

23. Are you ruminating about past events? What event(s)?

24. Are you thinking negatively? Can you switch to a positive mind frame?

25. Are you recovering from a bipolar episode? What positive steps are you taking to recover?

26. Do you get regular exercise?

27. Do you understand your bipolar legal rights?

28. Do you have a plan to win the war against bipolar disorder?

29. Do you understand what a whole-life wellness plan is?

30. Do you know how to optimize your medication?

31. Do you have a contingency (emergency) plan? Is it in writing?

32. Do you belong to a support group?

33. Do you trust your psychiatrist and/or therapist?

34. When is the last time you laughed?

35. What do you like to do for fun?

36. Are you financially stable and able to pay your bills?

37. When is the last time you made love?

38. Do you have good libido?

39. How well are your medications working? Do you need an adjustment?

40. Have you been diagnosed by a doctor? What is your diagnosis?

41. Do you have a Psychiatric Advance Directive?

Notes

Notes

—Troy Steven, Writer, Publisher, Aerospace Engineer

"Make a bipolar battle plan, be a warrior, and fight the war against bipolar disorder. Victory means living a productive, happy life—and making your dreams come true!"

Diagnosed with Bipolar Disorder

Chapter 1
What's At Stake

Your life could be at stake, and you may be your own worst threat. Studies show that up to 20% of people with bipolar disorder end their life by suicide, and 20-60% of us attempt suicide at least once in our lifetime. **It is unbelievably tragic that one out of five of us end our own lives!**

Other catastrophic outcomes of bipolar episodes can include:

- Physical violence
- Self-mutilation

- Financial disaster
- Loss of job and damage to career
- Loss of spouse or romantic partner
- Alienation of children
- Loss of friendships
- Loss of self-respect

Facts and Statistics.

The following facts and statistics are representative of research from a variety of sources, including both online and published material.

1. Bipolar disorder results in 9.2 years reduction in expected life span.
2. Approximately 25% of bipolar individuals are obese.
3. More than 40% percent of people with bipolar disorder struggle with alcohol and drug abuse.
4. Bipolar individuals are three times more likely to be diabetic than the general population.
5. Bipolar disorder and physical health are closely linked, with risk factors such as weight gain, metabolic syndrome, smoking, and diabetes contributing to cardiovascular disease and early death.
6. Bipolar disorder affects approximately 5.7 million American adults, or about 2.6 percent of the US population age eighteen and older in a given year.
7. Three of the top methods of bipolar suicide are guns, suffocation by hanging and poisoning by overdose.

8. Approximately 15 percent of people with bipolar disorder have had a violent episode. Bipolar individuals are prone to agitation that may result in impulsive aggression (as opposed to premeditated aggression) during manic and mixed episodes. However, depressed states, which can involve intense agitation and irritability, also carry a risk of violent behavior.

9. Bipolar disorder doesn't discriminate by age, race, ethnicity, or social class. It affects as many men as women.

10. There are many factors leading to medication non-adherence in psychiatric patients, including lack of insight into having an illness, distress associated with side effects affecting quality of life, lack of family and social support, insufficient information on the disease and treatment, and substance abuse or addiction.

11. There are many treatments and strategies that a person can use to manage their bipolar symptoms.

12. Bipolar disorder is not curable. **However, it is treatable.**

Notes

Notes

—Ted Turner, Media Mogul

"Winners never quit and quitters never win."

Diagnosed with Bipolar Disorder

Chapter 2
The Good Stuff

Take heart in the fact that when bipolar episodes are not occurring, individuals with bipolar disorder are busy living their lives, often excelling at their professions, being moms, dads, or students, just like anyone else. In fact, many bipolar individuals currently living or who have lived in the past will be remembered as successful individuals who left legacies of greatness and fame.

The following is a list of recognizable individuals who overcame their bipolar illness and achieved greatness and notoriety.

Ludwig Van Beethoven; Russell Brand; Drew Carey; Jim Carrey; Dick Cavett; Winston Churchill; Kurt Cobain; Salvador Dali; Jean-Claude Van Damme; John Denver; Charles Dickens; DMX; Richard Dreyfuss; Patty Duke; Carrie Fisher; Larry Flynt; Harrison Ford; Vincent Van Gogh; Halsey; Ernest Hemingway; Kay Jamison; Billy Joel; Meriwether Lewis; Abraham Lincoln; Kristy McNichol; Marilyn Monroe; Isaac Newton; Florence Nightingale; Jane Pauley; Edgar Allan Poe; Theodore Roosevelt; Brooke Shields; Ben Stiller; Sting; Ted Turner; Mark Twain; Mike Wallace; Robin Williams; Owen Wilson; Virginia Woolf; and Catherine Zeta-Jones.

List three of the individuals above who inspire you the most.

____

____

____

Remember these are only some of the people who are brave enough to admit that they are bipolar or are known to have coped with symptoms of bipolar disorder. Millions suffer daily, struggling alone, oftentimes afraid to confess to others or confront their condition. Too many go unnoticed and untreated until it's too late.

Positive Personality Traits Common to Bipolar Individuals:

Creativity: The link between bipolar disorder and creativity is well established. Visual arts, performing, written expression, and music—bipolar talent in all of the arts is common and sometimes exceptional.

Exuberance: Exuberance is an abounding, ebullient, effervescent emotion. It's a celebration of the passion and joy in mania and hypomania. It's contagious, starting with that person who makes everyone smile.

Emotional Perspective: What goes up must come down—and then go back up again. Viewing life and issues from both ends makes bipolar individuals more philosophical about the meaning of things. It also gives them a point of reference they didn't have before that people who lack the perspective of the ups and downs will never understand.

Depth of Experience: You will not meet more experienced, well-traveled, multidimensional people. They have exceptional and often unusual stories to share. People with bipolar disorder, who are so often adventurous, tend to be high achievers and leaders with above average intelligence.

Hyper-sexuality: Lust is also a prominent feature of mania. People with bipolar disorder tend to be dazzling, passionate, and adventurous lovers.

Depression: Surely you are wondering—what can be positive about depression? Light needs shadow, and the most profound understanding includes both. People with bipolar disorder are complex and can illuminate the whole human experience.

Resilience: After suffering through tragic bipolar episodes, bipolar individuals' act of resurrecting themselves gives them the resilience to handle almost anything else that may come their way throughout life.

Courage: Tied in with bravado and grandiosity, at its most severe, courage can entail dangerous risk-taking. Yet at its best, courage is rare, inspiring, and heroic.

Which of the personality traits above are your best strengths?

____

____

____

Notes

Notes

—Winston Churchill, 41st British Prime Minister
"Without victory, there is no survival."

Believed to have had Bipolar Disorder

Chapter 3
Create Your Bipolar Battle Plan

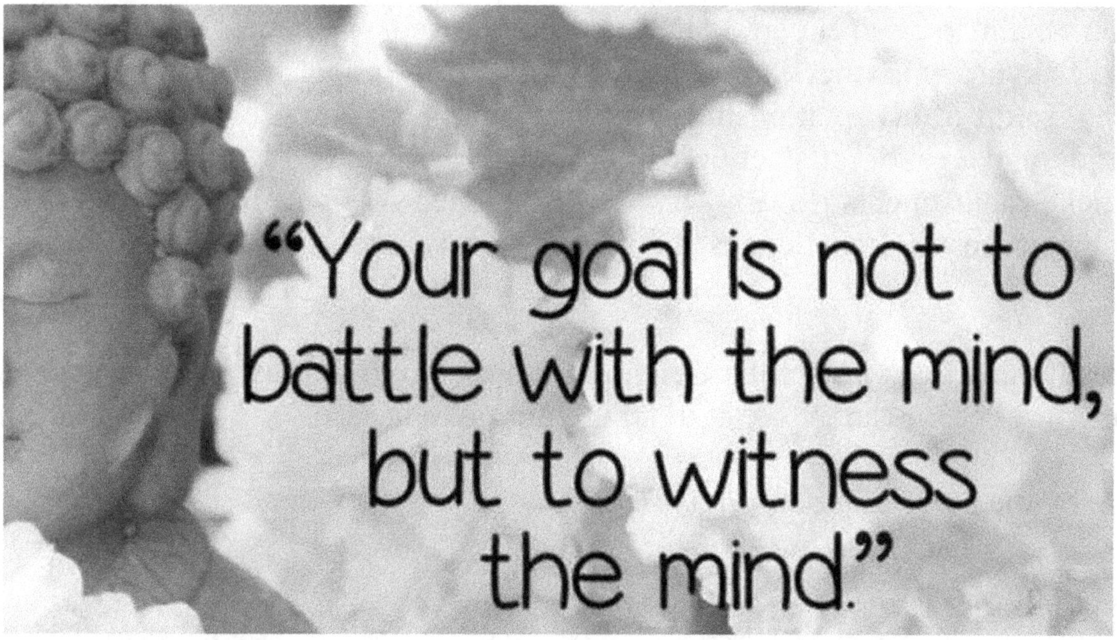

How do we battle a mental illness that has the ability to take control of our thoughts and emotions and cause our minds to deceive and betray us? How do we overcome an illness that has the power to cause us to attempt suicide, become violent, and spend money recklessly, not to mention act in so many other destructive ways? How do we surmount the health issues attributed to bipolar disorder such as a shorter life span, obesity, diabetes, and abuse of drugs and alcohol?

The best solution is to follow a lifelong battle plan that is based upon the expert recommendations of the medical community. The consensus is that successful treatment of bipolar disorder depends on diligently following a comprehensive treatment plan including medication, educating yourself about the illness, communicating with your psychiatrist and therapist, having a strong support system and helping yourself by making healthy lifestyle choices. This workbook gives you that plan.

This chapter guides you through the process of creating your personal bipolar battle plan. It explains the planning process, how to establish your goals and objectives, enemy reconnaissance, selecting your weapons, warrior training, and becoming a bipolar warrior.

I don't claim to be an expert. I make decisions based on whether I am experiencing bipolar symptoms, the state of my mental and physical health, financial well-being, status of my relationships with my significant other, children, family, and friends, and level of satisfaction with my job and my career. If changes are needed, I make adjustments to my battle plan. Each of you will have different circumstances and challenges than I do, so you should tailor your battle plan accordingly.

Bear in mind that you are the General of your own individual bipolar battle plan. You must become an expert at treating your own disease.

Live by the motto, *Bipolar Heal Thyself.*

The Planning Process

Planning ahead is how we deal with most challenges in life. Understanding the planning process will aid you in creating your battle plan. The planning process is shown in the figure below:

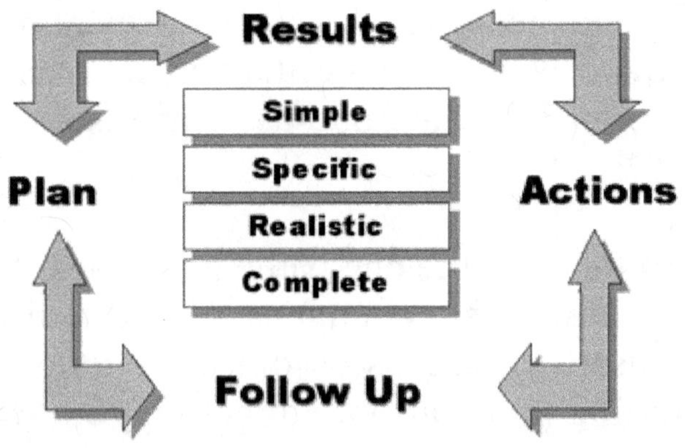

As you go through the process of creating your bipolar battle plan, ask yourself the following questions:

1. Is the plan simple? Is it easy to understand and to act on? Does it communicate its contents easily and practically?

2. Is the plan specific? Are its objectives concrete and measurable? Does it include specific actions and activities?

3. Is the plan realistic? Are the goals realistic? Nothing stifles implementation like unrealistic goals.

4. Is the plan complete? Does it include all the necessary elements?

Even if it passes all of these criteria, you will need to refine and make improvements to your battle plan on an on-going basis, depending on what is working for you and what is not working. The success of your plan depends on your level of commitment and involvement, as well as your ability to adapt to changing circumstances.

You are engaged in an undertaking of major importance to you. To be sure of success you must have plans that are faultless. If the first plan which you adopt does not work successfully, replace it with a new plan, if this new plan fails to work, replace it with still another. And so on. Be persistent. Your achievement can be no greater than your plans are sound.

Establish Your Goals and Objectives

The first rule of combat is to believe in your reasons to fight, which are your goals and objectives. This is the key: you have to believe that you WILL win. Not that it will happen, but that it should happen and that you are in charge.

When establishing your goals and objectives, consider your deepest wants and desires, your dreams, and what you want to achieve before leaving this great earth. *Don't limit yourself—you deserve the best of everything.*

Consider the following questions when setting your goals and objectives

1. What motivates me?

2. What interests me?

3. What would I do more of if I could?

4. What do I care about?

5. Where do I want my life to go?

6. What brings me joy?

7. What are my dreams and desires?

The goals and objectives I set for my bipolar battle plan include:

Bipolar Battle Plan Goals and Objectives
Effectively deal with bipolar symptoms or side effects
Eliminate bipolar episodes
Never attempt suicide
Maintain strong mental and physical health
Establish lasting financial security
Be in a romantic relationship with love on both sides
Foster good relationships with my family and friends
Do whatever it takes to make my dreams come true
Laugh out loud on a regular basis

Know Your Enemy

"Know your enemy and know yourself and in a 100 battles you will never be in peril."

—Sun Tzu, The Art Of War

Bipolar disorder is a very complex disease. It's also very serious and life-threatening. The more you know about bipolar disorder and how it affects you, the better you can manage and overcome the illness.

This chronic illness is best described as a mood disorder. It causes unusual and dramatic shifts in mood, energy, and the ability to think clearly. The mood of someone who is bipolar rotates between polar opposites: at one end of the spectrum are the highs (mania) and at the other end are the lows (depression). The most identifiable bipolar symptoms are these polar mood swings, each of which can last anywhere from days to weeks.

Bipolar disorder can look very different in each person. The symptoms vary widely in their pattern, severity, and frequency. However, bipolar disorder can also be somewhat predictable. For each person, the disorder tends to follow a pattern or can have some consistency. Within the broad groupings of manic and depressive symptoms, each person will have their own markers, or unique expressions of the illness that help to define their specific brand of bipolar disorder. For example, you may notice racing speech and thoughts, prolonged periods of irritability or anger, decreased need for sleep, or delusions of grandeur.

Recognizing that you are having similar symptoms to ones you experienced during past bipolar episodes can be a huge advantage if you are able to take evasive action sooner rather than later.

As you become familiar with your illness, you can learn your own unique patterns of behavior. If you learn to recognize these signs and seek effective and timely care, you can often prevent additional episodes. *Recognizing and naming your typical bipolar symptoms is the first important step to understanding and beginning to take control over your bipolar disease.*

Select your Weapons

For those of us who are bipolar, it is important to understand that we are facing a highly complex situation, and we can't hope to change it until we arm ourselves with the necessary psychological and intellectual capacity.

The weapons you select to include in your arsenal can be thought of as strategies, techniques, tactics, and knowledge you can deploy as needed to battle the enemy, your bipolar disorder. Choose your weapons based on the advice of the experts in the medical community, knowledge of the illness from past experiences, and the specific challenges that you currently face.

The nine weapons I selected to include in my battle plan for fighting the war against bipolar disorder are shown in the following figure:

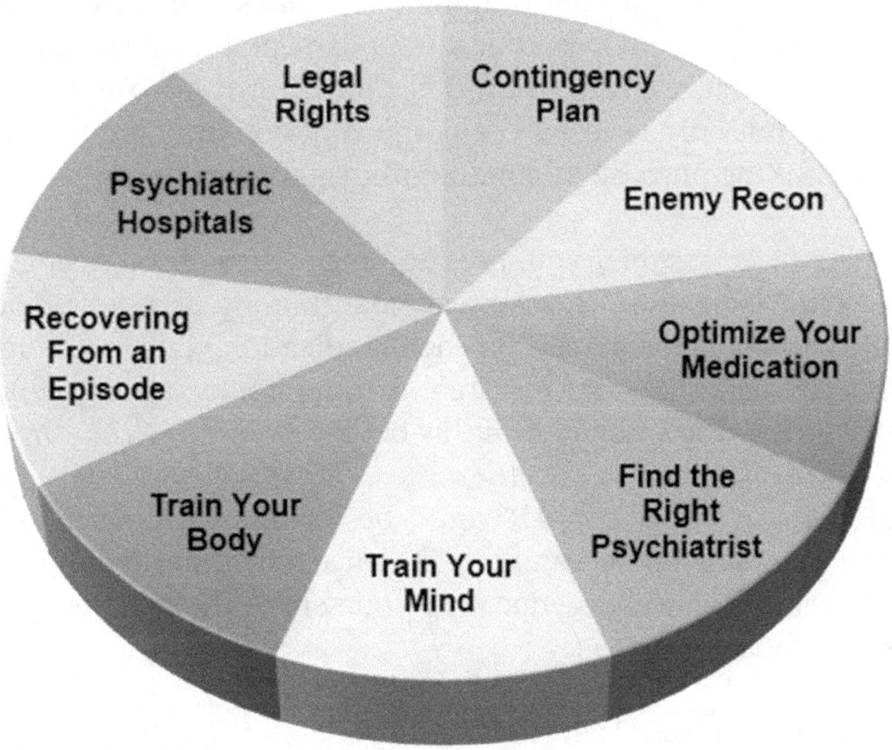

WEAPONS IN MY BIPOLAR BATTLE PLAN

All significant life changes take patience and commitment in practicing the new principles and skills. You must become an expert at treating your own disease.

Live by the motto, *Bipolar Heal Thyself.*

"*There is no such thing as tough; there's trained and there's untrained.*"
—Denzel Washington, Man on Fire

Bipolar Warrior Training

Now that you have selected your weapons for fighting the war against bipolar disorder, it is time to begin your training. Your objective is to become skillful in the use of each weapon and to master the fundamental technical and tactical skills necessary for warfare. This includes conditioning your mind and body. Conditioning is not only used for the purpose of conditioning for something, but it is also used for the purpose of conditioning against something.

For example, let's assume you are training yourself on using the weapon "Optimize your Medication." First, break your training into steps. The first logical step would be to educate yourself on each medication you are taking, or thinking about taking, by using internet research, reading books, asking your psychiatrist questions, and studying Chapter 6 of this book.

Additional steps in your training would be to gain proficiency in rating your medications, ramping up or ramping down a medicine, dialing-in the perfect medication cocktail, as well as educating yourself on the reasons why people stop taking their medicine.

Attributes of the Bipolar Warrior

"*The hardest thing in the world is to assume the mood of a warrior. It is of no use to be sad and complain and feel justified in doing so, believing that someone is always doing something to us. Nobody is doing anything to anybody, much less to a warrior.*"

—Carlos Castaneda

Warcraft of all types must be mastered. Developing expertise and proficiency in fighting the war against bipolar disorder is paramount for everyone with this sometimes devastating illness. I am giving you a call to arms to become a bipolar warrior. Fight, claw and scratch with all of your strength, courage, and willpower to overcome the bipolar beast that invades your mind and wants to destroy you. This is the most difficult and important undertaking you will ever face! No one deserves a negative kind of life, and I am passionate in my belief that it should not happen to you or to anyone else.

Ingrain this list of attributes of a bipolar warrior into your mind and incorporate them into your daily routines in order to successfully fight and win the war against bipolar disorder.

A Warrior:

- Knows that this is a battle for their life
- Understands the will to conquer is the first condition of victory
- Never accepts the unacceptable
- Makes a plan to defeat the enemy
- Knows that no plan survives first contact with the enemy
- Knows that wars are won on strategy, not impulse
- Knows that until they understand exactly what is going on and how to stop it, the most important weapon in their arsenal is reason
- Remains calm and in control at all times
- Knows that every minute lost in war can be the cause of defeat
- Makes up their mind to overcome struggles and challenges
- Adopts the mindset of a warrior every morning when they wake up
- Always do their best
- Prepares for battle

- Knows they are in a war with the parasite in their mind
- Fights with all their might
- Makes a plan and sticks to it
- Takes action to further their plan on a daily basis
- Focuses on what they can control
- Knows that once they face down the enemy, they are able to accommodate or even work with them
- Rolls with the punches
- Knows their strengths and weaknesses
- Avoids being taken by surprise
- Knows that even a badass needs rescued every once in a while
- Practices vigilance
- Learns as much as possible and knows information is power
- Voices and directs daily intentions
- Respects their enemies
- Knows that sometimes they have to change things up
- Trains their mind
- Trains their body
- Shores up their defenses wherever needed

- Eats healthy and stays hydrated

Precious moments have already been snatched from your life and the enemy will only try to steal more—if you allow it. Make the decision to win the war against bipolar disorder **NO MATTER WHAT**. Victory means living a productive, happy life—and making your dreams come true!

On the following page answer the following questions:

How has Bipolar Disorder tried to take away your happiness or life goals?

Which warrior attributes do you intend to add to your toolbelt?

Which attributes are you already feeling confident about mastering?

Notes

Notes

—Abraham Lincoln, 16th President of the United States
"A wise man once told me to always have a contingency plan."

Believed to have had Bipolar Disorder

Chapter 4
Make A Contingency Plan

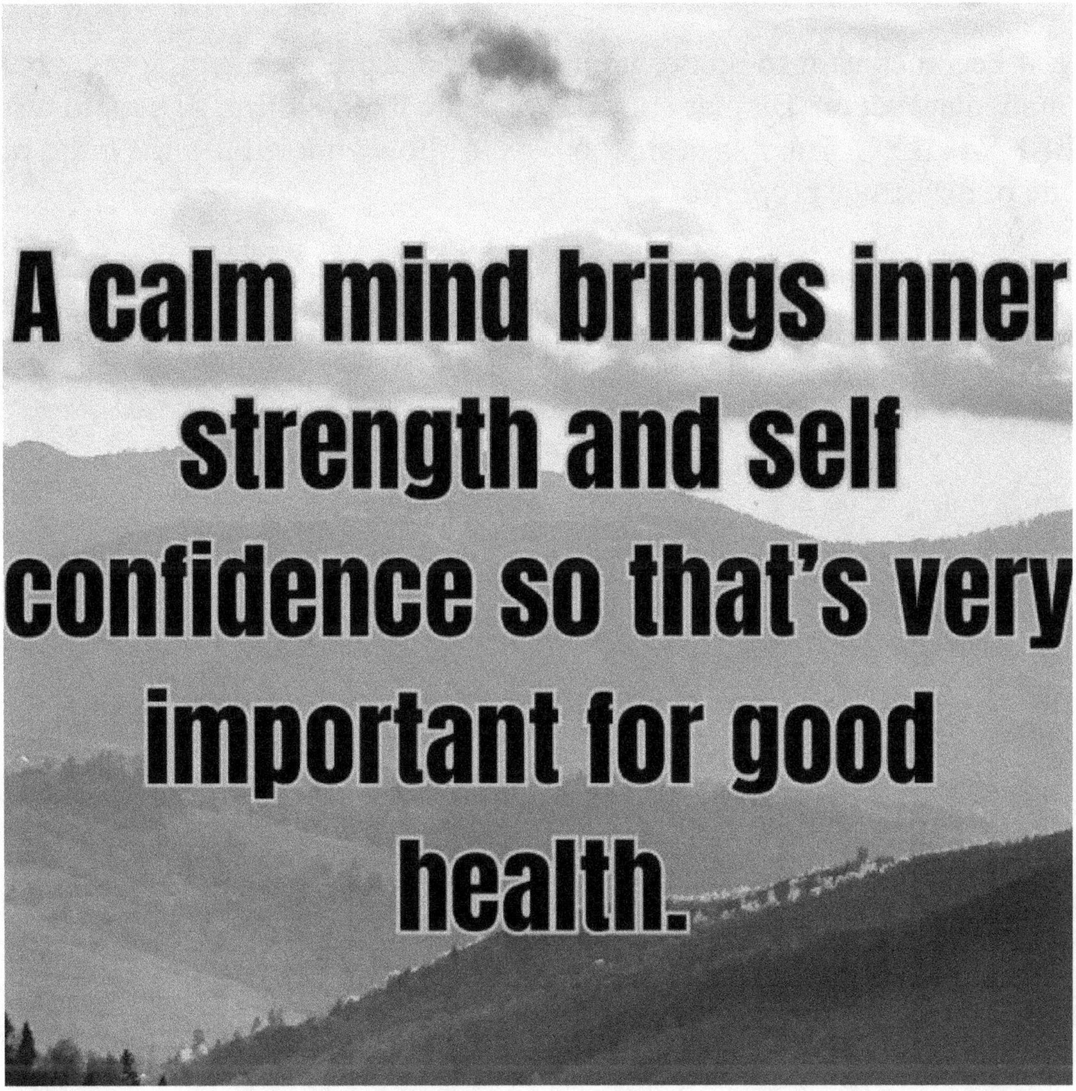

"Every military disaster can be explained in two words: too late."
–Douglas MacArthur

The contingency plan is one of the most important weapons of the overall battle plan. The purpose of the contingency plan is to keep you alive, out of the hospital, and out of jail when you are having a bipolar episode. It is the last line of defense to keep a manic episode from skyrocketing out of control or a depressive episode from plummeting to disaster.

When it becomes hard to ignore your manic or depressive symptoms, you must take immediate action. Bipolar episodes escalate like wildfire, so a rapid response is **EVERYTHING**. The stakes are too high to allow yourself to slide into a bipolar episode of disastrous proportions.

Select the items on the next page you want to include in your personal contingency plan.

Contingency Plan Actions
Ensure I am getting sufficient sleep
Make an appointment with my psychiatrist
Call the people who are part of my contingency plan
Distance myself from loved ones if I am agitated
Start taking my medications if I am not taking them
Stop drinking alcohol and doing drugs
Exercise and get fresh air
Stay hydrated
Take vitamins and eat healthy

Use this form to create your contingency plan. Think of it as your emergency plan.

Name: ____________________
Phone: ____________________
Address: ____

Support Team: **Name** **Phone Number**
Support Person 1 ____
Support Person 2 ____
Support Person 3 ____
Support Person 4 ____

24-Hour Emergency Numbers:

1) Immediate Emergency	Call 911
2) National Suicide Prevention Lifeline	1-800-273-8255
3) Mental Health Hotline	1-844-549-4266
4) Substance Abuse and Mental Health Helpline	1-800-662-4357
5) Crisis Text Line	Text 'HOME' to 741741

Current Medications:
1)
2)
3)

Medication Contingency Plan:
1)
2)
3)

Things That May Trigger a Relapse:
1)
2)
3)

Mania Early Warning Signs:
1)
2)
3)

Depression Early Warning Signs:
1)
2)
3)
If I develop any of these signs, I will:
1)
2)
3)
If my support people observe these signs, they may:
1)
2)
3)
These people can visit me in the hospital:
1)
2)
3)
I have a Psychiatric Advance Directive:

YES____ NO____

If "YES" attach it or note where it can be located. If "NO" one should be created in case of emergency.

Signature: ______________________________

Date: ______________________________

Remember to make a few copies of your Contingency Plan and give them to the people in your support team.

A PLAN IS USELESS IF NOT PUT INTO ACTION!

Notes

Notes

—Theodore Roosevelt, 26th President of the United States

"At sometimes in our lives a devil dwells within us, causes heartbreak, confusion, and troubles, then dies."

Believed to Have Had Bipolar Disorder

Chapter 5
Enemy Recon: Understanding Bipolar Disorder

Enemy Reconnaissance – Sikorsky Raider Helicopter

This chapter provides a detailed understanding of the true nature of the enemy, bipolar disorder. This includes:

- What is Bipolar Disorder?
- Bipolar Disorder is a Biological Illness
- Five Types of Bipolar Disorder
- Mania Early Warning Signs
- Common Symptoms of Mania
- Common Symptoms of Hypomania
- Depression Early Warning Signs
- Common Symptoms of Depression

- Bipolar Disorder Triggers
- Sleep Disturbances
- Causes of Bipolar Disorder

This Murderous Cauldron

"In a rage I pulled the bathroom lamp off the wall. I see in the mirror blood running down my arms, collecting into the tight ribbing of my beautiful, erotic negligee, only an hour ago used in passion of an altogether different and wonderful kind. I can't help it, I chant to myself, but I can't say it; the words won't come out, and the thoughts are going by far too fast. I bang my head over and over against the door. God, make it stop, I can't stand it. I know I'm insane again. I can't think, I can't calm this murderous cauldron, my grand ideas of an hour ago seem absurd and pathetic, my life is in ruins, and worse still—ruinous; my body is uninhabitable. It is raging and weeping and full of destruction and wild energy gone amok. In the mirror I see a creature I don't know but must live and share my mind with. I understand why Jekyll killed himself before Hyde had taken over completely, I took a massive overdose of Lithium with no regrets."

The above excerpt from the book *An Unquiet Mind* by Kay Jamison illustrates the changes in mood that intensify as a bipolar episode progresses. Kay goes from having "grand ideas" to an hour later feeling like she is "insane again" and her body is "uninhabitable." When a bipolar episode has progressed to this state there is nothing that can stop you from crashing and burning except getting help. Fortunately, Kay was rescued from this suicide attempt and continues her career as a professor of psychiatry at the Johns Hopkins University School of Medicine, as well as being a renowned author of books on mental illness. I highly recommend her national bestseller *An Unquiet Mind.*

What Is Bipolar Disorder?

Bipolar disorder is a very complex disease. It's also very serious and life-threatening. The more you know about bipolar disorder and how it affects you, the better you can manage and overcome the illness.

Bipolar disorder is a chronic illness that is best described as a mood disorder. This mental illness causes unusual and dramatic shifts in mood, energy, and the ability to think clearly. The mood of someone who is bipolar rotates between polar opposites: at one end of the spectrum are highs (mania) and at the other end are lows (depression). The most identifiable bipolar symptoms are these polar mood swings, each of which can last anywhere from days to weeks. Not everyone's symptoms are the same, and the severity of mania and depression can vary. Some people have "mixed states" in which they feel both mania and depression at the same time.

The mood swings seem to be triggered by things such as stress or change of seasons, so control of these triggers is possible. When mood swings occur, they affect how people think, act and feel. They can interfere with normal functioning, and they can make people act in uncharacteristic ways. The methods for catching and controlling mood swings help you learn new skills for identifying mood symptoms early in their development and use strategies for gaining control of these symptoms. Learn to recognise symptoms coming and find out how to take quick action to prevent making matters worse and to reduce your symptoms instead. Make it your goal to continually strengthen your coping skills so that you can take control of your mood swings.

A common misconception is that people believe themselves to be bipolar due to experiencing the everyday ups and downs of life. The difference in being bipolar is that these feelings are experienced in a much more drastic and dramatic way.

Some people alternate between extreme episodes of mania and depression, but most are depressed more often than they are manic. People with bipolar disorder may also go for long stretches of time without symptoms. However, the condition is usually cyclical, so be prepared for it to worsen and then improve at times. For those of us who live with bipolar disorder, this means accepting that mood swings and episodes of mania or depression will always be a potential challenge for us.

My dad was bipolar in the extreme but never admitted it or took medicine to control it. He would become manic and be high as a kite for several weeks, usually heading to Las Vegas or Atlantic City to gamble heavily. During his manic periods, he was busy managing his bar business, playing poker, attempting to start other businesses, and enjoying life. These periods of mania were essentially the driving force behind his success as an entrepreneur. They also backfired through causing him to gamble large sums of money in careless ways. I remember the positive factors associated with his manic episodes most. He would talk to my sisters and I and become involved with our lives. The times when he was depressed were far worse. He would sit in his La-Z-Boy watching television in his robe, day after day, week after week, uncommunicative and down in the dumps. He kept the bar running, and the only other thing he paid attention to was the television. These depressed periods of time were much longer than the manic periods of time. Having witnessed the detrimental effects of bipolar disorder on my dad, I vowed not to let bipolar disorder disrupt my life as much as it did his.

It is important to educate yourself on all aspects of bipolar disorder, just like you would do if you were going to have a major operation such as brain surgery or kidney replacement. Study the subject as if you are getting a Master's degree in Bipolar Disorder. Never stop learning.

In her book *Madness: A Bipolar Life*, Marya Hornbacher captures the essence of bipolar disorder:

> *"Here's the hell of it: madness doesn't announce itself. There isn't time to prepare for its coming. It shows up without calling and sits in your kitchen. You ask how long it plans to stay; it shrugs its shoulders, gets up, and starts digging through the fridge. In the early years, it's like a switch flips on, and though only a moment before you were totally sane, suddenly you have gone mad. But as you learn to manage madness, you begin to notice sooner that it's on its way."*

Bipolar Disorder is a Biological Illness

Like heart disease or diabetes, bipolar disorder is a biological illness and most often, medication is required to treat it. Medication can bring your mania and depression under control and prevent relapses once your mood has stabilized. Bipolar disorder has a number of different symptoms, reflecting difficulties in several different areas or systems of the brain. Different medicines target separate brain functions. You may need medicines to help stabilize your mood, curb manic symptoms, relieve depressive symptoms, help you sleep, manage anxiety, control psychosis, improve information processing, or compensate for side effects.

Bipolar disorder can affect a person's energy level, judgment, memory, sleep patterns, sex drive and self-esteem. Bipolar disorder has also been linked to anxiety, substance abuse, and health problems such as diabetes, heart disease, migraines, and high blood pressure. You may be asking yourself *What doesn't bipolar disorder affect?*

Five Types of Bipolar Disorder:

The medical community has defined five types of bipolar disorder which are used to diagnose people with the illness and determine treatment plans accordingly.

Bipolar I Disorder (Mania or a Mixed Episode)

Bipolar I Disorder is the classic manic-depressive form of the illness in which you have a period of abnormally elevated or irritable mood, as well as extreme changes in emotions, thoughts, energy, talkativeness and activity level. This highly energized level of physical, mental activity, and behavior is a change from your usual self and is noticeable by others. This would last at least 7 days or be severe enough for hospitalization.

A mixed episode is when symptoms of depression and mania are experienced at the same time. This can lead to irritability, hostility, and physical aggression. Depending on the severity of the symptoms, patients may be hospitalized for their safety and the safety of those around them. They may need a longer hospital stay and a combination of more than one medication to get well.

Bipolar II Disorder (Hypomania and Depression)

This features both mania and depression, but the mania is less severe than in Bipolar I, and doctors call it hypomania. Hypomania is a less severe form of mania that does not last as long or happen as frequently, so it does not interfere with daily life as much. A person with Bipolar II may experience a major depressive episode preceding or following a manic episode.

Bipolar III (Cyclothymic Disorder)

This type includes symptoms of hypomania and depression that last for two years or more in adults or one year in children. These symptoms do not fit the criteria for wholly manic or depressive episodes.

Bipolar IV Disorder

In Bipolar IV Disorder, hypomanic and manic episodes come from taking antidepressant drugs. Doctors prescribe anti-depressant medication to treat other types of mental illness. Unfortunately, antidepressants are known to trigger bipolar disorder in many cases.

Bipolar V Disorder

This subtype refers to patients who have a family history of bipolar disorder but only have symptoms of major depression themselves.

How is Bipolar Disorder Diagnosed?

Bipolar disorder is a complex condition, which can make diagnosis a difficult and lengthy process that can require a multidisciplinary team. Assessment typically begins by comparing one's lived experience with the DSM-5's classified bipolar symptoms. Additionally, the doctor will ask for a medical history, family history and may conduct a physical exam and order lab tests to rule out any other conditions.

Note: The DSM-5 is the diagnostic and statistical manual of mental disorders.

Do you know your diagnosis?

I have been diagnosed with Bipolar I ______

I have been diagnosed with Bipolar II ______

I have been diagnosed with Bipolar III ______

I have been diagnosed with Bipolar IV ______

I have been diagnosed with Bipolar V ______

Mania

Remember this rule of thumb if you are experiencing a manic episode: "What goes up must come down." Mania causes people with bipolar illness to climb higher and higher and then crash like a wave rolling into the shore.

Mania is defined as a state of abnormally elevated arousal and energy level. During a manic episode, an individual will experience rapidly changing emotions and moods, highly influenced by surrounding stimuli. The heightened mood can be dysphoric as well as euphoric. As the mania intensifies, irritability can be more pronounced and result in anger or anxiety.

The symptoms of mania include elevated mood (either euphoria or irritability), flight of ideas, pressure of speech, increased energy, decreased need and desire for sleep, and hyperactivity. In full-blown mania, these symptoms become progressively exacerbated. In severe manic episodes, these symptoms may even be obscured by other signs and symptoms characteristic of psychosis, such as delusions of grandeur, paranoid delusions or hallucinations. As a result, discernment is significantly reduced.

When experiencing mania, the bipolar individual is very productive, typically running around like there is never enough to do. They tend to be overly happy and optimistic about life. If a person has extreme manic episodes, hallucinations and psychotic symptoms are possible. Psychosis is a state in which a person is unable to tell the difference between reality and non-realistic states of mind. Psychotic symptoms may include hallucinations and false beliefs about having special powers or a special identity–such as believing you are God, have superhuman strength, or having X-ray vision. This can be a neat experience, with the mind offering escape through fantasy, but it is not reality.

During a manic episode, a person might impulsively quit a job, charge huge amounts on credit cards, or feel rested after sleeping a short time period. Manic symptoms can include minute-to-minute mood swings, rapid speech, grandiosity, impulsiveness, delusions, the feeling of complete invincibility, and the absolute conviction that certain untrue things are true.

Another symptom of mania called psychomotor agitation manifests itself as unintentional purposeless physical activities that arise from tension and anxiety. Someone may pace around a room, wring their hands, or make more dangerous motions such as ripping, tearing, or chewing at the skin.

Common early warning signs of mania
Answer Yes or No if you are having any early warning signs of mania.

Mania Early Warning Signs		
	YES	NO
Similar pattern of symptoms from previous episodes		
Heightened mood and over valued self confidence		
Sleep disturbances		
Suicidal thoughts		
Inflated sense of self-importance		
Increased physical and mental activity and energy		
Excessive irritability and aggressive behavior		
Racing speech and thoughts		
Impulsiveness, poor judgement		
Grandios delusions and hallucinations		

Mania Early Warning Signs		
	YES	NO
Hallucinations		
Argumentative, picking fights		
Increased sex drive		
Compulsion to talk incessantly, unsually sociable		
Jumping from one thought to another or project to project		
Aggressive or fast driving		
Impulsive purchases		
Reckless behavior and risk taking activities like gambling		
Feeling bullet proof or endowed with special powers		
Impatience or frustration with the slowness of others		

Common Symptoms of Mania

Answer Yes or No if you are having any symptoms of mania.

Symptoms of Mania		
	YES	NO
A long period of feeling overly happy		
Extremely irritable mood, agitation, feeling jumpy or wired		
Talking very fast, jumping from one idea to another		
Having racing thoughts		
Loss of touch with reality		
Being easily distracted		
Increasing goal-oriented activities		
Being restless		
Reduced need to sleep		
Having an unrealistic belief in one's abilities		

Symptoms of Mania		
	YES	NO
Behaving impulsively		
Taking part in high risk behaviors - spending sprees		
Risky business investments		
Having impulsive sex		
Unexplained aches or pains		

Hypomania

Hypomania is a less severe form of mania. People experiencing hypomania are able to carry on with their day-to-day lives and don't lose touch with reality. Keep in mind that hypomania can escalate to full-blown mania or be followed by a major depressive episode.

Common Symptoms of Hypomania

Answer Yes or No if you are having any symptoms of hypomania.

Common Symptoms of Hypomania		
	YES	NO
Having a higher or happier mood than usual		
Heightened irritability		
Rude behavior		
Feeling overconfident		
Higher activity or energy levels		
A powerful feeling of physical or mental well being		
More sociable or talkative than usual		

Depression

When most people think of bipolar disorder, they think of the manic side. However, depression is the far more common and more damaging of the two poles. In the euphoria of mania, people rarely choose to intentionally harm themselves. In a deep depression, however, self-mutilation and suicidal thoughts and actions are far too common.

Depression is a form of reversible brain failure. When someone is depressed, it's like their mental computer processing unit isn't working properly. As a result, focusing on a single idea or task is very difficult. Depression intrudes on their mind and fills it with negative thoughts.

Depressive symptoms may include dreariness, extreme pessimism, hopelessness, and lack of focus. People who are depressed may feel that their thoughts move slowly, take little pleasure in any activity, feel worthless and feel their lives are meaningless. They may stay in bed all day, feeling that they can't get going. They often isolate themselves from others. They may begin to overindulge with food and if they have low activity level, gain weight. They may speak or think about suicide or become violent, making emergency care crucial for their safety and others. In addition, psychotic symptoms may occur during severe depressive episodes.

Depression Early Warning Signs:
Answer Yes or No if you are having early warning signs of depression.

Depression early warning signs		
	YES	NO
Social withdrawal and isolation		
Increased feelings of worry and anxiety		
Little interest in sex		
Inability to concentrate or make decisions		
Unexplained aches or pains		
Slowed and difficulty thinking		
Paranoia		
Hallucinations		
Self-loathing		

Depression early warning signs		
	YES	NO
Similar pattern of symptoms from previous episodes		
Sleep disturbances		
Suicidal thoughts		
Abandoning activities you usually enjoy		
Not answering your phone or responding to email or texts		
Continually having negative thoughts		
Prolonged sadness or unexplained crying spells		
Loss of energy		
Changes in appetite		
Paying less attention to personal appearance and hygiene		

Common Symptoms of Depression:

Answer Yes or No if you are having symptoms of depression.

Common Symptoms of Depression		
	YES	NO
A long period of feeling worried or agitated		
Loss of interest in activities once enjoyed		
Thoughts of death or suicide		
Feeing tired or slowed down		
Having problems concentrating		
Having problems remembering		
Having problems making decisions		
Change in eating, sleeping or other habits		
Low Libido		
Unexplained Aches and Pains		

Common signs & symptoms of mania

- Showing intense happiness or silliness
- Having a very short temper or seeming extremely irritable
- Talking very fast or having racing thoughts
- Having an inflated sense of ability, knowledge, and power
- Doing reckless things that show poor judgment

Common signs & symptoms of depression

- Feeling very sad or hopeless
- Feeling lonely or isolating from others
- Eating too much or too little
- Having little energy and no interest in usual activities
- Sleeping too much

Use this worksheet to track your Bipolar Symptoms over time:

SYMPTOM TRACKER

DATE	TIME	DURATION	DESCRIPTION

Seasonal Pattern

Seasonal pattern describes mood disorders that are triggered by a particular season of the year. For example, someone who tends to become manic during the spring and summer and then returns to a regular mood during the late fall and winter has a seasonal pattern of mania. Alternatively, someone who tends to become depressed during the late fall and winter and then returns to a regular mood during the spring and summer has a seasonal pattern of depression. The fall/winter depression pattern is more common than the spring/summer pattern. Suicide is far more common in March, April and May probably due to changes in light.

Pay attention to your moods during different seasons of the year and determine if you have a seasonal mood pattern. If so, you can adjust your treatment plan accordingly.

Bipolar Episode Triggers

Triggers are outside events that can launch new episodes of mania or depression or cause existing bipolar symptoms to worsen. Triggers are the main environmental causes of mood swings and need to be monitored and eliminated. One of the best ways to prevent future episodes is to identify and avoid the specific triggers that ignite your bipolar symptoms. Lack of sleep, going off of your medications, alcohol and drug use, and major stress are some of the top triggers that set off a bipolar episode.

Scott talks about two bipolar triggers he has learned to avoid:

"I used to get stressed out whenever I traveled back to Indiana for family gatherings at my mom and dad's. A couple of years ago, I came back home from visiting my parents over the Christmas holidays and ended up having a bipolar episode and sinking into depression for a couple of months. I figured out that the two biggest stress factors for me during these visits were being around a large group of people and not having my own place to retreat. I still go home to visit but not during the holidays. I go when I can visit with just a few people at a time. Also, I stay in a hotel instead of staying at my mom and dad's place. Since I made these two changes, my last two visits have been enjoyable."

For each of us, our stressors and triggers are different. Identifying the triggers that may set you off can help you to avoid an episode. Once you identify your personal triggers, you can work on recognizing them as they occur and handle them more effectively.

Identify the stressors in your life and learn powerful techniques for dealing with these stressors to assist you in developing the skills for recreating your life in a more balanced and joyful way. It will help you to be healthier and more productive at work and in your personal life.

Learn to avoid the events and circumstances that may trigger you to have a bipolar episode. If something triggers you, promptly launch your Contingency Plan.

Common Triggers of Bipolar Episodes:
Answer Yes or No if you have any of these triggers in your life.

Common Triggers of Bipolar Episodes	YES	NO
New relationships		
Lack of exercise		
Birth of a child		
Travel and jet lag		
Feelings of loneliness and dispair		
Non-supportive family or friends		
A death in the family		
Stress at work		
Change in environment		
Taking on more than you can handle		
Loss of employment or changing jobs		
Thyroid malfunction		

Common Triggers of Bipolar Episodes		
	YES	NO
Sleep Irregularities		
Financial Problems		
Increase in stress		
Isolation		
Stopped taking medication		
Alcohol or drug abuse		
Side effects from medication		
Change of seasons		
Forgetting to take medicine		
Taking on more than you can handle		
Conflict with others		

Sleep Disturbances

Getting sufficient sleep is CRUCIAL if you are bipolar. Sleep disturbances are a key symptom of both mania and depression and an excellent early warning sign of a mood change. Your ability to get a good night's rest is highly influenced by the circadian system, which is the body's twenty-four-hour internal biological clock. The circadian rhythm of your body determines when you need sleep and when you need to wake. It is through this rhythm that your body knows when to start and stop certain chemicals in your brain.

To put it simply, regulated sleep stabilizes the brain chemicals that control emotions. Maintaining a consistent sleep schedule and wake time can help you avoid nighttime sleeplessness or daytime exhaustion, therefore decreasing the risk of new episodes of mania or depression.

Regulating sleep is often one of the best ways to balance moods and the circadian system. When you go to sleep easily, sleep and dream deeply, and then wake up refreshed on a set schedule every day, you're experiencing regulated sleep.

Unfortunately, maintaining a regular sleep schedule is not always as easy as it sounds, especially if your neighbors, family, roommates, schedule, lifestyle, or sleeping arrangements do not cooperate. The more you upset the natural circadian rhythm by working odd hours, staying out late and partying, ignoring what you put into your body, or watching upsetting television before bedtime, the less likely you are to find stability. You may need to change some of these behaviors in order to kick your circadian rhythm into gear so that you can sleep more soundly and therefore give your brain and your body time to recharge. Sticking to a sleep routine, winding down with pre-bedtime rituals, reducing caffeine intake, and getting your family or roommates to cooperate can prove to be very helpful.

Common Contributors to Unregulated Sleep

Answer Yes or No if you have any of these contributors to unregulated sleep.

Common Contributors to Unregulated Sleep		
	YES	NO
Shfit work, ever changing schedule		
Stress		
Drugs and Alcohol		
Caffeine		
Travel to different time zones		
Life changes		
Frisky Bed Partner		
Bright light before bed		

Bipolar Disorder Is Somewhat Predictable

What is your bipolar modus operandi? Bipolar disorder can look very different in each person. The symptoms vary widely in their pattern, severity, and frequency. Some people are more prone to either mania or depression, while others alternate equally between the two poles. Some have frequent mood disruptions, while others experience only a few over a lifetime.

However, bipolar disorder can be somewhat predictable. For each person, the disorder tends to follow a pattern. It surprisingly has some consistency. Within the broad groupings of manic and depressive symptoms, each person has their own markers or unique expressions of the illness that help to define that person's specific brand of bipolar disorder. For example, you may notice racing speech and thoughts, prolonged periods of irritability or anger, decreased need for sleep, or delusions of grandeur.

As you become familiar with your illness, you can learn to recognize your own unique patterns of behavior. If you learn to self-recognize these recurring signs and seek effective and timely care, you can often prevent additional episodes. Recognizing and naming your typical bipolar episode symptoms is an important first step to understanding and taking control of your bipolar disease.

Each of the five bipolar individuals I interviewed for this book reported that their bipolar episodes had similar characteristics. John, Scott, and Ruth's episodes start with mania, whereas Gary and Jane's episodes start with depression. Also, the symptoms they experienced were comparable between episodes. This applies to my bipolar episodes as well. John and Scott describe the similarities between their episodes below.

John describes the symptoms he experienced at the onset of his past bipolar episodes:

"*At the beginning of my bipolar episodes, I become more expansive, feel more in tune with other people, and don't sleep as much. A common symptom of mine is attributing hidden meanings to things that happen and what people say, even if I just overhear conversations. Another symptom I experience is hearing God talking directly to me telling me what to do. These days I keep tabs on what I am thinking and monitor my mood on a regular basis. If I notice any of these symptoms, I know I better do something fast because an episode is brewing."*

Scott has also learned to monitor himself closely for symptoms based on previous episodes:

"My bipolar episodes always begin on the manic side. There is a critical juncture in time where I realize that I am having off-the-wall thoughts, or other symptoms, and I know I need help. At this point in time, I usually make an attempt to get help by calling my psychiatrist. However, if I don't talk to him or see him that day, it's too late, game over. I become more and more obstinate. My mania grows exponentially and gathers steam like a runaway freight train without any brakes."

Causes of Bipolar Disorder

The exact cause of bipolar disorder is unknown. It is not clear whether it may lie dormant in the brain and be activated on its own or be triggered by environmental factors such as social circumstances, psychological stress, abuse, significant loss, imbalanced hormones, or traumatic experiences.

Experts believe bipolar disorder is partly caused by an underlying problem with specific brain circuits and functioning of brain chemicals called neurotransmitters. The brain is made up of billions of nerve cells called neurons that move a constant stream of information from one to another. Chemical messengers in the brain known as neurotransmitters transmit signals between neurons. Neurotransmitters play a crucial role in emotional health, are involved in brain functions, and also help in the functioning of the human body. The abnormal brain circuits identified in bipolar brains are believed to cause certain neurotransmitters in the brain to be dysfunctional.

Neurotransmitters

Scientists have identified serotonin, dopamine, and norepinephrine as the three prevalent neurotransmitters involved in mood regulation, stress responses, pleasure, reward, and cognitive functions such as concentration, attention, and executive functions. When the levels or density of these neurotransmitters are not at a normal level, the result can be the manifestation of bipolar disorder.

Serotonin is a brain chemical that is connected to several body functions such as wakefulness, sleep, sexual activity, eating, learning, impulsivity, and memory. Any abnormal rise or fall in the serotonin levels of the human brain can lead to mood disorders, which elevate medical conditions such as bipolar disorder.

Dopamine has consistently been linked with the part of the brain that controls the human pleasure center. This neurotransmitter helps control body movements and patterns of thought, while also regulating how hormones are released. Abnormal dopamine activity in individual's brains may explain the symptoms of bipolar disorder.

Norepinephrine plays a role in cognition, mood, emotions, movement, and blood pressure. Imbalance in norepinephrine causes difficulty concentrating, fatigue, anxiety, apathy, and depression.

Research on Bipolar Disorder

Positron Emission Tomography (PET) is a brain-imaging technique that has been used to measure the monoamine density of cells that release the brain chemicals dopamine, serotonin, and norepinephrine. By performing PET scans in areas of the brain in which monoamine-releasing cells are concentrated, an approximate 30 percent increase in density of these cells was found in the brains of bipolar people even when not having symptoms. The altered brain chemistry due to excessive monoamine cells directly affects cognitive and social functions.

Studies continue to determine which kinds of monoamine cells are involved in producing serotonin and norepinephrine. Those findings could help define specific subtypes of bipolar disorder and aid in the development of medications and drug combinations that target a specific patient's personal brain chemistry to alleviate symptoms.

Magnetic resonance imaging (MRI) technology has been used to view the brains of individuals with bipolar disorder. The results of these studies showed gray-matter abnormalities in various regions of the brain. Gray matter is a major component of the central nervous system, consisting of neuronal cell bodies. Scientists have found gray matter deficits in the ventromedial prefrontal regions of the bipolar brain (located in the rear of the front part of the brain, inside the cortex and atop the orbits of the eyes), and in the anterior limbic cortices of the brain. The particular brain areas affected with gray-matter deficits impact certain brain functions. The ventromedial prefrontal regions of the brain affect concentration, inhibition, emotions, behavior, learning, and the anterior limbic cortices affect smell, agitation, emotional control, and memory.

By studying the gray matter found in the brains of bipolar and non-bipolar individuals, scientists hope to correlate the volume of gray matter with the duration of bipolar illness and the number of episodes.

Genetic Predisposition

Bipolar disorder has a strong, but as-of-yet unknown tie to DNA. There is an overwhelming amount of evidence that bipolar disorder can be inherited. The evidence for a genetic predisposition to bipolar disorder is so strong that based on studies of twins, an estimated 80 percent of the risk is inherited. If one of your parents or siblings has the disorder, your chances of having bipolar disorder are four to ten times greater than they would be if no one in your family has it. In conclusion approximately 33 percent of children who have a parent with bipolar disorder will contract the disease.

Gary comments on the possibility that his kids may have inherited bipolar disorder:

"Are you kidding me? Having to deal with my bipolar disorder is hard enough without worrying my kids may also have it. I have talked to each of my kids about my illness. They have witnessed how the disease affects me, visited me in the hospital, and have been around me when I was manic or depressed. I pray that none of my children are bipolar with all of my heart!"

Scientists are trying to find specific genes that are involved in causing bipolar disorder in hopes of finding genetic markers that will provide knowledge of an individual's risk of developing the disorder. A combination of both genetic research and neuroimaging studies are being pursued to help define both the genetic components of this illness and their relationship with specific brain markers that define a chemical fingerprint of bipolar patients.

The important thing to remember is this—what's inherited in bipolar disorder is not the illness itself but vulnerability. Whether someone does or does not get the illness depends on what is happening in that person's life. Interventions like medications or family support that reduce stress and introduce structure to someone who is vulnerable to bipolar illness can be very helpful and may prevent or delay the onset of the illness.

Notes

Notes

—Catherine Zeta-Jones, Actress
"She's got herself worked out with her meds and she's raring to go!"
(Quote from Husband Michael Douglas)

Diagnosed with Bipolar Disorder

Chapter 6
Optimize Your Medication

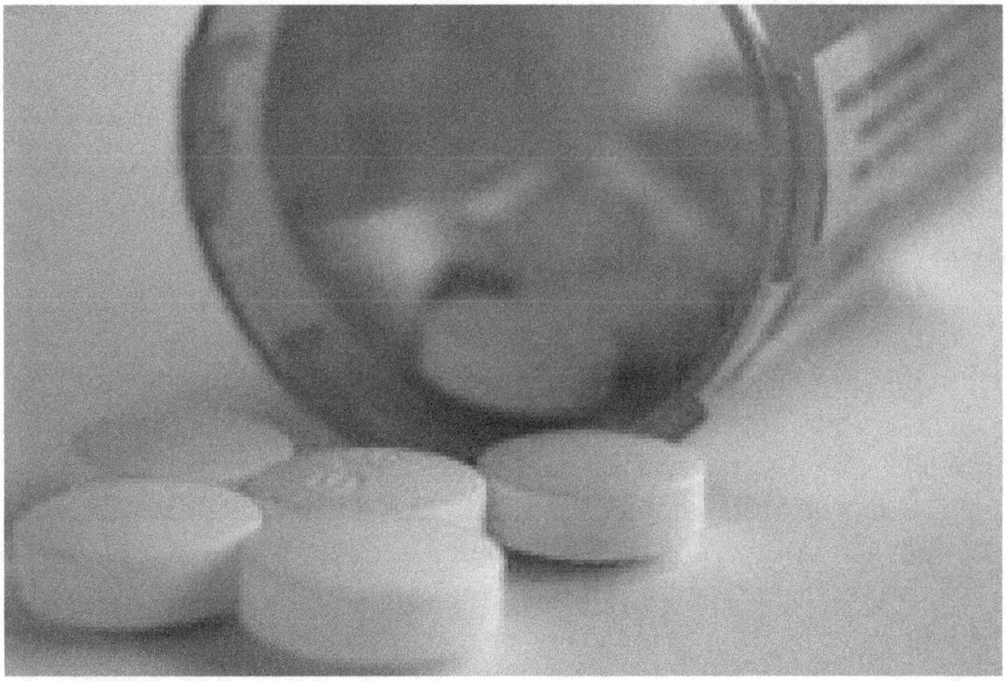

In this chapter you will learn how to determine the best medications and corresponding dosages to effectively battle your bipolar illness and achieve optimal mental and physical health.

This chapter discusses:

- The role of medication in treating bipolar disorder
- Bipolar heal thyself
- Getting the most out of bipolar medications
- Researching your medications
- Becoming your own mental detector

- Rating your medications
- The perfect medication cocktail
- Beware of side effects

Learning how to determine the best medications to treat your bipolar illness is imperative and can be one of your most powerful weapons in fighting the war against bipolar disorder. Your psychiatrist will prescribe your medications, but you are the only one who can tell if they are working effectively. You must become an expert at treating your own disease.

Bipolar medications are most effective when used in conjunction with therapy and healthy lifestyle choices, which can affect the amount of medication required and help manage symptoms without side effects. Finding the right drug can be tricky, so it's important to work closely with a specialist and re-evaluate your medication regularly as the optimum dose may change over time.

It takes skill, finesse, and guts galore to determine the specific medications that will effectively combat your bipolar disorder. Just as it takes time and practice to learn golf or a new language, learning how to use the powerful pharmaceutical medications to effectively treat your bipolar illness is a skill that improves with experience. It is your job to push the limits of your medications in order to find the sweet spot where you are mentally sharp and focused, have plenty of get up and go, a positive attitude, no bipolar symptoms, and are happy with yourself and your life.

You do not want medications to make you feel mediocre; you want them to make you feel great!

The Role of Medication in Treating Bipolar Disorder

If you have bipolar disorder, medication will likely be the foundation of your treatment plan. Medication can bring mania and depression under control and prevent relapses once your mood has stabilized. You may not like the idea of taking bipolar medication long-term, especially if you're struggling with unpleasant side effects. But just as a diabetic needs to take insulin in order to stay healthy, taking medication for bipolar disorder will help you maintain a stable mood.

Be aware that you should not expect medication alone to solve all your problems. There are plenty of other steps you can take to manage your symptoms and reduce the amount of medication required. Medication is most effective when used in combination with other bipolar disorder treatments, including therapy, self-help, coping strategies, and healthy lifestyle choices.

Bipolar Heal Thyself

Strive to find the best combination of medicines to treat your illness, just as heart patients or cancer patients search for the right medicines to treat their disease. Learn how to rate your medications and tweak the dosages based on how you feel both mentally and physically.

While medication is typically the foundation behind bipolar disorder treatment, therapy and self-help strategies also play important roles. You can help control your bipolar symptoms by exercising regularly, getting enough sleep, eating a heathy diet, monitoring your moods, keeping stress to a minimum, and surrounding yourself with supportive people and influences. Living with bipolar disorder is challenging. With medication, healthy coping skills, and a solid support system you can live fully while managing your symptoms.

Optimizing your medications includes researching your medications, becoming your own 'mental detector,' dialing-in your medications, ramping up and ramping down your medications, learning the possible side effects of each of your medications, and understanding the reasons why people stop taking their medications.

Getting the Most out of Medications for Bipolar Disorder

Take advantage of natural mood stabilizers. Your lifestyle has an impact on your symptoms. If you make healthy daily choices, you may be able to reduce the amount of medication you need. Mood stabilizers that don't require a prescription include keeping a strict sleep schedule, exercising regularly, getting plenty of sunshine, practicing relaxation techniques, and developing a solid support system.

Add therapy to your treatment plan. Research shows that people who take medication for bipolar disorder tend to recover much faster and control their moods better if they also get therapy. Therapy gives you the tools to cope with life's difficulties, monitor your progress, and deal with the problems bipolar disorder is causing in your personal and professional life.

Continue taking medication, even after you feel better. The likelihood of having a relapse is very high if you stop taking your bipolar medications. Suddenly stopping medication is especially dangerous. Talk to your doctor before you make any changes, even if you believe you no longer need medication. Your doctor can help you make any adjustments safely.

Finding the Right Bipolar Disorder Medications. It can take a while to find the right bipolar medications and dosages. Everyone responds to medication differently, so you may have to try several bipolar disorder drugs before you find the one or combination that works for you. Be patient, but don't settle for a medication that doesn't work or makes you feel lousy either.

Once you've discovered the right bipolar disorder drug or drug cocktail, it may still take time to determine the optimal dose. In the case of mood stabilizing medications, the difference between a beneficial dose and a toxic one is small. Continue taking your medication even after you feel better as the likelihood of having a relapse is very high. Frequent office visits to re-evaluate your bipolar medication needs in addition to careful monitoring of symptoms and side effects will help you stay safe.

Research Your Medications. Being aware of the pros and cons of any new medication is very important. Research each medication using online resources, the expertise of your psychiatrist, and by talking to other bipolar people who are or were taking the same medication.

For example, let's assume you are training yourself on using the weapon "Optimize your Medication." First, break your training into steps. The first logical step would be to educate yourself on each medication you are taking, or thinking about taking, by using internet research, reading books, and asking your psychiatrist questions.

Researching your medications
Fill in the answers to the questions below.

Research Your Medications
How will I know if the medications are working?
What are the expected results (pros) of the medicine?
What are the side effects and risks (cons) of the medicine?
What is the target dosage and therapeutic range?
What time of day should I take the medicine?
Are there foods or substances I need to avoid?
How will the drug interact with my other medications?
Is there someone I trust to give me feedback on the new med?

Become Your Own Mental Detector. Many diseases can be detected by some kind of medical test—for example, blood tests for diabetes and kidney function, or CT scans for brain tumors, but there is no test to specifically detect bipolar disorder. The telltale signs are bipolar symptoms, major mood changes, and bipolar episodes. This is why it is vital that you stay vigilant in monitoring and assessing your own moods and energy levels.

The onset of a bipolar episode is not readily apparent. Episodes start slowly, oftentimes unnoticeably, and they pick up speed as the days go on. You must be astute enough to recognize that you are experiencing bipolar symptoms and strong enough to take appropriate action. Because no one else knows your thoughts, feelings, and inherent behavior patterns like you do, it is crucial that you become your own "mental detector."

Monitor your thoughts, moods, and energy levels on a regular basis. Ask yourself the questions on the following page.

Are your medications working?
Answer Yes or No.

Be Your Own Mental Detector to Determine if Your Medications are Working	YES	NO
Have I laughed today?		
Do I feel like myself?		
Do I have a good libido?		
Am I looking forward to something in the future?		
Did I barely drag throughout the day?		
Am I having any psychotic thoughts?		
Am I displaying depressive or manic behaviors?		
Am I sleeping well?		

As soon as you notice bipolar symptoms, take action ASAP! Allow no delays, there is no time to lose.

Mood Log: A powerful tool is to track your mood using a Mood Log. The primary purpose of the Mood Log is to identify recurrence of symptoms when they are beginning. If you make a habit of rating your mood each day, you will know when changes occur and whether they are reactions to events or more persistent changes that signal a return of bipolar symptoms. This is a also helpful to communicate to your psychiatrist or therapist how you have been doing between appointments.

Use the form below to track your mood over time. This will help you to detect your mental state and take evasive action if needed.

Bipolar Disorder: Mood Log Worksheet

NAME.........................   WEEK.........................
..

Mood Tracking

Date	Mood (Morning)	Mood (Afternoon)	Mood (Evening)	Energy Level (1-10)	Sleep Quality	Triggers

Mood: Indicate your mood using a scale (e.g., 1-10, where 1 = very low/depressed, 10 = very high/elevated/manic).
Energy Level: Record your energy level on a scale from 1-10 (1 = very low, 10 = very high).
Sleep Quality: Note the number of hours and the quality of sleep (e.g., restful, disturbed).
Notes/Triggers: Include any events, thoughts, or activities that might have affected your mood.

Dial-In Your Medications. Dialing-in your medications to the optimal dosage is one of the most valuable skills to master. This is where the rubber meets the road. Most bipolar individuals take more than one medicine at a time and determining the 'medication cocktail' that works best takes time, patience, and skill. It's important to work closely with your psychiatrist and reevaluate your medication regularly, because the perfect dosage may change over time. Self-reflection, in addition to writing in a journal, can be very helpful to track your mood shifts from day to day.

In order to dial-in the optimal dosages of your medications, you must become proficient at researching the medicine, rating your medications, ramping the medicines up or down as needed, mixing the perfect medication cocktail, as well as educating yourself on the reasons why people stop taking their medicine.

Journaling your thoughts regarding any of these reflective questions can be quite helpful in determining the effectiveness of any medication. It is uncommon, if not impossible, for any medication to immediately change your life. Be patient!

The Perfect Medication Cocktail. You may have to try a number of different medicines before you zero in on the right medication cocktail that works best to treat your bipolar illness. Finding the right combination and dosages of medicines to effectively treat your bipolar disorder is a trial-and-error process that will most likely take a while. The perfect medication cocktail is different for every individual. To attain peace of mind, optimal brain functioning, good energy levels, and overall well-being, you need to keep experimenting with different medicine combinations and dosages until the results meet or exceed your expectations and criteria.

Just getting by is not good enough; settling for less than happiness is a cop-out. Life is short. The right combination of medicines can make you strong, happy, and whole again. Your heart will know when you have found the Holy Grail of medicines that make you glad you are alive!

As time goes by and you experiment with different medicines, you will become more proficient at dialing-in the medications to the optimum dosages for treating your illness. The biggest thing to remember is not to lose hope. You are working toward a better life, and your diligence and patience will pay off.

If all indications are that the medicine or combination of medications is a go, congratulations! You have successfully dialed-in your medications.

Beware of Side Effects. Any time you start taking a new medication, you must be on the lookout for side effects. A side effect is any unwanted, non-therapeutic effect caused by a drug. Most psychiatric medicines have side effects of one kind or another. Some people are prone to experience side effects from a particular medicine, while others do not experience any side effects at all from the exact same medicine. It is vital to watch out for side effects. Be wary because some side effects are more serious than others. Some side effects can actually kill you! Any psychiatrist worth their salt will inform you of the possible side effects when prescribing medication. If they don't warn you of the possible side effects of the medicine, then consider getting a new psychiatrist. You can also make a habit of automatically asking your doctor how the medication can negatively change or alter your state of being or for warning signs to look out for.

Side effects lie in wait like a lion stalking its prey until the medicine reaches a certain threshold in your bloodstream. Side effects may happen quickly or may occur several days after you begin taking the medicine, while some may not show up until much later. Take heed because this could be weeks or months after you start taking the medication. Everything may be going along smoothly, and then BAM! Things take a very drastic turn, and not in a good way.

If something is going wrong physically or mentally, always look to one of your medications as the possible culprit.

The three worst side effects that impacted me are:

- Instantaneous puking without warning
- Extreme trembling in my hands
- Erectile dysfunction

In each case I was able to pin down which medicine was causing the side effect and when I went off that medication the side effect went away (luckily). The erectile dysfunction took several months to manifest itself which made it tough to determine what medicine to go off of. This was not helpful in my marriage as you can imagine.

Some medicines have side effects that will taper off as your body gets used to the dosage level. For example, you may feel dizzy when you reach a certain dosage, but the dizziness goes away once you take that dosage for a few days. You will have to judge the seriousness of the side effect. If it is tolerable, see whether the side effect subsides.

The bottom line is that you must monitor yourself mentally and physically when you are taking any kind of medication. If anything unusual starts happening, immediately call your doctor and make an appointment.

General Side Effects of Bipolar Medications

Anser Yes or No if you are experiencing any of these side effects.

Side Effects from Medication	YES	NO
Agitation		
Anxiety		
Blackouts		
Constipation		
Drowsiness		
Excessive thirst / dry mouth		
Hallucinations		
Headaches		
Increased Urination		
Insomnia		

Side Effects from Medication		
	YES	NO
Loss of coordination		
Muscle stiffness / Pain		
Nausea / Vomiting		
Rashes or itching		
Sedation		
Sensitivity to the sun		
Sexual Dysfunction / Low Libido		
Tremors		
Weight gain		
Weight Loss		

Medicine Noncompliance

Caution: The top risk factor for relapsing into a bipolar episode is going off your medications.

There are a number of reasons why we who have bipolar disorder stop taking our medication:

- A manic episode begins and our thoughts go wild. We love the highs of being manic
- We don't think the medication is helping
- The medicine causes unwanted side effects
- We plan to start taking the medicine again if we experience any bipolar symptoms
- We want to be 'ourselves'
- We think we are smarter now that we have experienced a bipolar episode and can use our willpower to keep from having another.

In conclusion, when taking medication for your bipolar illness, persistently work with your psychiatrist to dial-in your medications so that you have good mental and physical health, no bipolar symptoms to speak of, and feel like a million bucks. Never give up.

Recommendations

1. It can be extremely detrimental to stop taking your medications, especially all at the same time. Two of my bipolar episodes escalated out of control when I stopped taking my medications. I ended up in the psychiatric hospital on both occasions.

2. Keep a close eye on your medications and don't let yourself run out or forget them if you go on a trip. It is easy to do and has happened to me more than

once. Going without my medications for even a couple of days will drastically mess with my mind. Also, I keep an extra set of daily medications in my vehicle in case I forget to take my pills in the morning.

3. If you don't have prescription insurance coverage, or even if you do, there are huge savings to be had by using GoodRx (www.goodrx.com). For example, I filled a prescription for 30 days of 400 mg tablets of Seroquel. Since I don't have prescription insurance it was going to cost $370. Fortunately, using GoodRx, it only cost me $17.

Notes

—Kay Jamison, Writer, Professor of Psychiatry

"No pill can help me deal with the problem of not wanting to take pills; likewise, no amount of psychotherapy alone can prevent my manias and depressions. I need both."

Diagnosed with Bipolar Disorder

Chapter 7
Choose the Right Psychiatrist

In this chapter you will learn:

- Criteria for rating a psychiatrist
- Typical questions to ask a psychiatrist
- Typical questions a psychiatrist may ask
- How to get the most out of appointments with your psychiatrist

- When you should consider getting a new psychiatrist
- Pointers on how to find a new psychiatrist

Finding a good psychiatrist is crucial to managing your illness and can be a powerful weapon in the ongoing war against bipolar disorder. A psychiatrist is a medical doctor who works to prevent, diagnose, and treat mental, emotional, and behavioral problems. A psychiatrist's medical training allows them to order medical tests and prescribe medication. Psychiatrists complete four years of medical school plus four years in a psychiatric residency program. Their education requires time spent in classrooms, medical offices, and hospitals—working directly with patients and other medical professionals. These are well-educated people devoted to helping others. But, again, not all psychiatrists have the same mindset.

Finding a psychiatrist who you trust to treat your bipolar disease and keep you healthy, alive, and out of the hospital is essential. The skills, abilities, and competence of your psychiatrist to repair, tune up, and maintain your mind can be likened to that of an auto mechanic who is the only person you trust to work on your car.

Remember, you are the customer paying a professional for their services. If your current psychiatrist isn't meeting your expectations, find someone who is better suited for your needs.

Choosing a psychiatrist is no easy feat because someone else's 'good' may not be good for you. Everyone is different. The best course of action is to research and interview a doctor—just like hiring an employee to work for you. While 'good' is different for each person, one thing remains the same: a good psychiatrist is one with whom you are happy. That's all. A good psychiatrist is one who performs to your expectations, whatever those may be.

The only way for a psychiatrist to help you is for you to be brutally honest with both them and yourself. Tell them about any bipolar symptoms you are having and what you are thinking and feeling. This will help them gauge how your medications are working and determine whether a change is warranted.

Rating a Psychiatrist

Here is a list of criteria that will help you find the right psychiatrist to treat your bipolar illness. Answer Yes or No.

Criteria for Rating Your Psychiatrist		
	YES	NO
They establish a contingency plan with you		
They tell you to call day or night if you need help		
They are skillful at determinging your state of mind		
You feel you can trust them		
You value their advice		
They are easy to talk to and make you comfortable		
They have several years of experience treating Bipolar		
They promote a whole-life wellness plan		
They are very knowledgeable about medication		
They explain the pros and cons of each medicine		

Criteria for Rating Your Psychiatrist		
	YES	NO
They tell you the side effects of each medication		
They explain the therapeutic range of each medication		
They are knowledgeable about new research on Bipolar		
They answer your questions without judgment		
They are covered by your insurance		
They are board certified		
They won't put up with nonsense		
They have hands on experience in psychiatric hospitals		

Typical Questions a Psychiatrist Might Ask:

Typical Questions a Psychiatrist May Ask
How's your mood?
Are you having any bipolar symptoms?
How are your medications working for you?
Are you experiencing any side effects?
Are you sleeping well?
How's your energy level?
How's your job?
How's your sex life?
Have you been exercising and eating healthy?
How are your releationships with family and friends?

Typical Questions to Ask a Psychiatrist:

Typical Questions to ask a Psychiatrist
What if I have an emergency outside of office hours?
Have you worked in a psychiatric ward or hospital
How do you decide what medications your patients take?
How often do you see your patients?
How long are appointments?
How much does an appointment cost?
What is your typical treatment plan?
What is your view on supplements and alternative medicine?
What is your view on psychotherapy?
What percentage of your patients have Bipolar Disorder?

Getting the Most Out of Appointments

Prior to having an appointment with your psychiatrist, it is smart to prepare in advance what you want to discuss and accomplish. When the appointment begins, your psychiatrist will try to gauge how you are doing and your state of mind. If you are manic, depressed, experiencing noticeable bipolar symptoms, or side-effects, tell your doctor. Keeping your true thoughts or feelings a secret from your doctor will only harm you in the long run.

After questioning you about your mood and state of mind, your psychiatrist will ascertain what dosage you are taking of each of your medications. Then they will assess your medication regimen and decide, based on your input, whether to make a change in the dosage of one of your current medications, or counsel you in regards to going off a medicine or starting a new one. Before the appointment, decide whether your current medicine regimen is optimizing your potential or you feel that a change is needed. If the medicine is not working, be prepared to state the reasons why. Keeping a Mood Log is very helpful. The more specific you can be, the better your doctor can treat your condition. If you feel strongly that you need a change in your medications, then stick to your guns.

Ruth relates how she prepared for a recent appointment with her psychiatrist:

"A few days before my scheduled three-month appointment with my doctor, I thought about how things were going in my life. I considered my mental state, energy level, relationships, last time I made love (too long), and how my job and career were going. My conclusion was I was too much of a wimp. I wasn't meeting any guys, although I'm fairly attractive. In general, I wasn't pleased with my personality, I was too laid back and not very sociable. When I met with my doctor, I asked him what changes I could make with my medications to be more assertive. He told me to decrease the dosage I was taking of Depakote from 750 mg a day to 400 mg."

Your psychiatrist is not in charge of what medications you take. You are! The doctor prescribes medication for you and then will make modifications based upon your feedback. It is your responsibility to keep making changes to your medications until you find the perfect medication cocktail for optimum mental and physical health. It's your life, your brain, and your happiness that are at stake. Keep working with your psychiatrist to find the medications that make you whole. Continue making adjustments to your medications until you are happy with the results.

Notes

—Isaac Newton, Physicist, Mathematian

"I can calculate the motion of heavenly bodies, but not the madness of people."

Believed to have had Bipolar Disorder

Chapter 8
Train Your Mind

This chapter discusses:

- The path with heart
- Self-importance is your greatest enemy
- Stop the internal dialogue
- Positive and negative emotions
- Process of autosuggestion
- Death is stalking you
- Stalk yourself
- Face fear head on
- Running the Bipolar marathon

"*We either make ourselves miserable, or we make ourselves strong. The amount of work is the same.*"

-Carlos Castaneda

Your mind is your most powerful weapon. Your thoughts are the only thing over which you can exert complete control. What you think and believe becomes a reality and rules your life. However, for those of us who are bipolar, it is a paradox that we must use our mind to fight a disease that at times has the power to take control of it.

Learning strategies and techniques to strengthen your mind will improve brain power, increase emotional well-being, decrease stress, and bring happiness and joy to your life. This chapter includes strategies from several self-help gurus such as Napoleon Hill, Miguel Ruiz, Carlos Castaneda, and others.

The Path With Heart

"*Anything is one of a million paths. Therefore, a warrior must always keep in mind that a path is only a path; if he feels that he should not follow it, he must not stay with it under any condition. His decision to keep on that path or to leave it must be free of fear or ambition. He must look at every path closely and deliberately. There is a question that a warrior has to ask, mandatorily. Does this path have a heart. A path without a heart is never enjoyable. On the other hand, a path with heart is easy—it does not make a warrior work at liking it; it makes for a joyful journey; as long as a man follows it, he is one with it*." -Carlos Castaneda

Regarding making decisions in our lives as to what paths to follow and what paths to avoid, the above words of Carlos Castaneda ring true and cannot be refuted. Use your heart as a GPS to guide you in the direction of your dreams. You will know when you are achieving the results you are striving for when your heart leaps for joy. A path with heart is formed by deliberately selecting a number of things that you want to involve yourself with regarding relationships, vocations, hobbies, arts or anything that connects your heart with the world. The criteria for selection are peace, joy, and strength.

Always Do Your Best

"I do the very best I know how, the very best I can, and I mean to keep doing so until the end."

—Abraham Lincoln

Doing your best in everything you do is a habit you can groom—the more you practice, the better you get. By consistently doing your best, your life improves dramatically, your self-respect increases, and so does your productivity. Doing your best is about taking action and doing what you love to do because your life will consist of actions that make you happy.

"Always do your best. For sure, you can always do your best. And your best changes all the time—when you are sick or tired, your best is different than when you are awake and fresh. But by always doing your best, you are going to be content with yourself. If you make the choice to do your best and believe it, that is your best. You have the power to make the choice. And magic begins to happen in your life. This is the mastery of life. This is the path to personal freedom.

Under any circumstance simply do your best and you will avoid self-judgment, self-abuse and regret. Everything you have ever learned you have learned by repetition. You learned to write, to drive, and even to walk by repetition. Practice makes the master. By doing your best you become the master. If you do your best always, over and over again, you will become a master of transformation."

—Miguel Ruiz

I know when I truly believe I have done my best. I feel accomplished in new ways. I am able to unclutter my mind and redirect my energy into the next logical step or task that I should take, as well as set goals and actively reach them.

Do your best every day and be proud of yourself for your efforts. When you haven't done your best, forgive yourself, quickly move on, and commit to trying harder next time. Make doing your best a daily challenge in your life. If you approach a task, even something as minute as tying your shoes, with the mind-set that you are going to do it right the first time, it will keep you from spending the time redoing it. As the saying goes, time is money. If you do your best over and over again, you will enrich your life, become more productive, and improve your self-esteem.

Self-Importance Is Your Greatest Enemy

Self-importance is the belief that you are more important than everyone else. Exaggerating one's importance is often accompanied by arrogance, conceit, and egotistical behavior. Think about it. Our self-importance causes us to be offended by other people in terms of what they say, and what they do. This is a huge waste of energy and our precious time. It weakens us.

Here are some questions to help avoid taking things personally. Answer Yes or No.

Am I Taking Things Too Personally?		
	YES	NO
Is it really about me?		
Could there be another explanation?		
Is it possible it has nothing to do with me?		
Is it about another person?		
Is it important enough to worry about?		
Am I just being overly sensitive?		

Are you exhibiting these traits of self-importance? Answer Yes or No.

Self-Importance Causes Us To:		
	YES	**NO**
Feel offended		
Defend our image		
Complain		
Reject ourselves		
Suffer needlessly		
Feel sorry for ourselves thru exaggerated self-pity		
Think negatively		
Make everyone else wrong		
Defend our opinions		
Gossip about ourselves or others		

How much time do we spend complaining about our problems, feeling offended about something someone said or did, or feeling sad and playing 'Poor Me' through victimization? It is easy to play the guilt card, especially while experiencing symptoms from mental illness! But it is not worth it.

For example, you spend all day thinking about a girlfriend or boyfriend who upset you, whether you should stay with them, and wondering if you are wasting your time with this person. That night, you get into a car accident, and the last thought you have before you die is, "Man, I wasted the whole day feeling lousy when I should have been having fun, enjoying myself, and being thankful for just being alive."

Don't take yourself so seriously. Reducing self-importance frees up energy that can be rechanneled into furthering your goals, decreases negative thought patterns, eliminates needless anger and suffering, and increases happiness.

To free mental and emotional energy, annihilate the self-important patterns of behavior such as the presentation and defense of the self in everyday life, excessive routines, the tremendous insistence on the concerns of the self, and the incessant preoccupation with romantic courtship.

Stop the Internal Dialogue

The internal dialogue is the incessant voice in our heads that has been programmed and groomed to focus on our egos ever since we started to think. Our minds constantly focus on our internal dialogue, known as self-talk. Our self-talk programs and shapes our self-concept. For example, if you believe you are worthy and strong, you will live up to that truth. On the other hand, if you criticize yourself and tell yourself you will never accomplish what you want, you won't. Conditioning yourself to stay in a positive mind frame does wonders for your overall mental health.

Autosuggestion

In his best-selling book *Think and Grow Rich*, Napoleon Hill explains a process called autosuggestion, which relies on the principle, "What you focus on, you attract."

Autosuggestion is the process of voluntarily fixing your attention upon a definite major purpose of a positive nature and forcing your mind through daily habits of thought to dwell on that subject.

The dominating thoughts that you hold in your conscious mind act to magnetize your subconscious, and these 'magnets' attract the forces, people, and circumstances of life that you desire. This is why visualizations and affirmations can have such a powerful effect in your life.

The language of the subconscious mind relies on feelings and emotions. Emotions are either positive or negative; both cannot occupy the mind at the same time. By focusing on positive emotions and banishing negative ones, you save up energy to expend on your definite major purpose instead of wasting your energy on negativity.

There are seven positive emotions and seven negative emotions that your subconscious understands:

Positive Emotions:	**Negative Emotions:**
Desire	Fear
Faith	Jealousy
Love	Hatred
Sex	Greed
Enthusiasm	Vengefulness
Romance	Superstition
Hope	Anger

The process of autosuggestion consists of the following steps:

1. Decide on a major purpose you really want to accomplish.

2. Say this intention out loud every day: "My subconscious mind is my partner in success."

3. Concentrate on your major purpose and visualize what it will look and feel like when it comes true.

4. Flood your mind with positive emotions.

5. Stay alert and receptive of the ideas, people, and circumstances that show up in your life to aid you in the achievement of your major purpose.

6. Take action.

7. Spend ten minutes every day for a month following the above steps.

It is important to remember that taking steps to set your intentions is only effective if you make a consistent effort and you work toward putting your words into action.

Death Is Stalking You

"*Time waits for no man.*"
—Abraham Lincoln

A warrior uses death as their most important advisor. Warriors routinely ask the following questions:

- If all I have is this moment, how do I want to use it?
- Is this the best I can do?
- Is this activity worthy of my life?
- If I died right now, would my death respect me?

"*In a world where death is the hunter, there is no time for regrets or doubts. There is only time for decisions. Our most costly mistake as average men is indulging in a sense of immortality. It is as though we believe that if we don't think about death, we can protect ourselves from it. Only the idea of death makes a warrior sufficiently detached so that he is capable of abandoning himself to anything. He knows his death is stalking him and won't give him time to cling to anything, so he tries without craving all of everything.*"
—Carlos Castaneda

Using death as an advisor helps you to focus on what matters most and also makes things clear. Other concerns pale in comparison. Meaning wells up from your heart and you gain clarity on how you want to spend your time and live your life.

The following words from the movie "*Walk the Line*" about the life of Johnny Cash highlights the importance of using death as an advisor:

"*All right let's bring it home. If you was hit by a truck, and you were lying out in that gutter dying, and you had time to sing one song, one song people would remember before you're dirt, one song that would let God know what you felt about your time here on earth, one song that would sum you up, are you telling me that's the song you'd sing, that same Jimmy Davis tune we hear on the radio all day, about your peace within and how it's real and how you're gonna shout it? Or, would you sing something different, something real, something you felt? 'Cause I'm telling you right now that's the kind of song people want to hear. That's the kind of song that truly saves people. It ain't got nothing to do with believing in God, Mr. Cash. It has to do with believing in yourself.*"

As I write this section in a Starbucks, a spry-looking lady of about sixty barely escaped slipping on the wet concrete outside, having a nasty fall, and perhaps splitting her skull. Luckily, she caught herself. Death is always a stone's throw away. Our time on earth is limited, and there is no time to be mediocre. Embrace your own essence and grab life by the horns!

Stalk Yourself

The "Art of Stalking" is a set of procedures and attitudes that enables you to get the best of any conceivable situation. For this discussion, stalking results in positive results and is not associated with doing any kind of harm to other people.

A friend of mine told me about a conversation he had with his son about the art of stalking:

"*My twenty-year-old son and I were sitting in a booth at Denny's waiting for his girlfriend to show up. He was getting irate because she was late. We reminisced, as we always did when the subject of being late came up, about his mom (my ex), who was habitually late and drove me and the kids crazy. He kept looking at his watch, and I knew he was going to jump his girlfriend's case when she arrived.*

He calmed down when I asked him when he had to leave and go to work. He said he had an hour so there was no big hurry. I asked him if he had ever heard about stalking someone, not in the sense of intending to do them harm or being a predator, but in terms of gaining energy and not wasting it. He said, "No, what do you mean?" I explained that the art of stalking is a set of procedures and attitudes that would enable him to get the best of any situation.

I told him an example of stalking would be to not act irritated to his girlfriend when she arrived—don't show any negative emotion at all but convince her it doesn't bother you one bit that she is late. If she says she is sorry for being late, simply say, "No problem, I don't have to leave for work for a while." I explained to him that acting in this manner, even when he was irritated on the inside, would keep him from wasting his energy being negative, would prevent her from feeling bad, and help us have a much better time eating breakfast together. By following this course of action, he would have successfully stalked her because she would treat him better and be more understanding when he did something that pissed her off.

Then I drove home the most important benefit of stalking. I told him that by stalking his girlfriend, he was actually stalking himself. By using his mind in a disciplined manner and choosing not to take her arriving late personally, he wouldn't cause himself or anyone else at the table needless suffering and save himself from expending energy unnecessarily."

It feels strange to think of stalking yourself, doesn't it? Try it and see how effective it can be.

"*Because your mind is especially subject to the dominating influences in your environment, you must take control over those influences by developing beneficial mental habits. The process of controlling your habits is miraculous. It translates the power of thought into action. But if your habits are poor or bad, they can bring misery and failure. Your success depends on the strength and quality of your controlled habits."*

-Napoleon Hill

Stop Defending Your Self-Image

Over the years you have built an idealized self-image that you defend as your sense of self. In this image are packed all the things you want to see as true about yourself; banished from it are all the shameful, guilty, and fear-provoking aspects that threaten your self-confidence. People spend a lot of time in therapy trying to turn a bad self-image into an acceptable one. As reasonable as that sounds, all self-images have the same pitfall: they keep reminding you of who you were, not who you are. The whole idea of I, me, and mine has been erected on memories, and these memories are not really you. Focus on the present and your sense of you will be the updated, positive one you want and desire.

Stop Trying to Make Others Wrong

To conserve energy, stop trying to make yourself right and others wrong. Everyone is a product of their environment and has formed an opinion about almost everything. If you stop caring whether you are right or wrong, then you will stop judging yourself and others and trying to prove that your opinion is superior to theirs. Most importantly, you will stop wasting your energy.

Accept Yourself

We are our own worst enemies due to the habit we have of criticizing and judging ourselves. We criticize ourselves a hundred times a day without even realizing it. Think about it—how often do you give yourself a hard time over past events, things you said, or past actions? The more emotion that was invested in the event, the more we criticize ourselves for the same transgression over and over again. Reduce the amount of time you spend criticizing yourself, and your mind will be more at peace.

Erase Personal History

For most people, personal history must be constantly renewed by telling parents, relatives, friends, and coworkers everything that we do or that happens to us. As a result, they pin us down with their thoughts and expectations. Erasing personal history frees us from the encumbering thoughts of other people. We are not defined by our past—the future is what matters.

Start keeping personal things to yourself that you normally would share with someone else. Slowly over time, tell people less and less about what you do and who you are. In this manner, you can begin to erase your personal history. Camouflage your personal history to keep from being pinned down by other people's thoughts or expectations. You need not be pigeonholed because you are bipolar, for example.

The benefits of erasing your personal history include:

- No one pins you down with their thoughts or expectations
- You can re-create yourself into whomever you want to be
- Forgetting the past allows you to focus on what is happening now and stop wasting your energy mulling over past events

Explanations are a sign of weakness. With every explanation, there is a hidden apology. An average man believes that his explanations of life will enable him to survive, but explanations are a meaningless waste of time. Understanding is a matter of experience, not the result of explanations. By erasing personal history, no explanations are needed, and nobody is angry or disillusioned with our acts.

Face Fear Head On

"Courage is being scared to death but saddling up anyway."
—John Wayne

Anytime you come up on something and the only thing that keeps you from doing it is fear your decision is automatically made. You therefore look your fear straight in the eye and proceed in that direction.

Too often we allow fear, worry, and doubts to dominate and define our lives. We allow them to steal our joy, our sleep, and our precious dreams.

Your emotional posture is a major influence regarding how others relate to you and how you experience the world. If you're afraid of doing something, you're likely to avoid it or be timid doing it. At the same time, if you don't acknowledge negative feelings, you allow them to fester and thus diminish physical, mental, and emotional health. Worry, for example, warps energy. Enmeshed in the furrows of worry, people constantly struggle with and tear apart stabilizing energies such as control, patience, and timing. Thus, people become accessible and lose their balance and their wits.

There are several steps you can take to face fear:

1. Get comfortable with fear.

2. Make your dominant thoughts positive.

3. Don't give attention, energy, or time to fear.

4. Don't dwell on scarcity.

5. Laugh at your fear.

6. Tell yourself that in one hundred years, whatever happens as a result of you facing your fear won't matter.

7. View life as a wild adventure.

Plan to be great.

A powerful technique that can help you face fear is to visualize a positive end result and consider steps you can take until you know exactly what you need to do to succeed. For example, many of us are afraid of public speaking. In order to face that fear, set your intention by planning your speech in your mind and then writing it down. Next, practice, practice, and practice in front of a mirror while visualizing the speech going smoothly and on course as planned. When you first walk up in front of your audience, pause and take three breaths before you begin to speak. When you begin to talk, say something funny. The audience will relax, and so will you. Finally, instead of standing still and not moving while delivering your speech, recite a paragraph and then move to the left or to the right a few steps and continue.

I used the above advice when I spoke at my Dad's funeral. Writing the speech down was the key, as well as practicing in front of a mirror. The end result was that I was able to honor his life and felt grateful for being able to do so.

Positive Thinking

Operate on the premise that it takes the same amount of work to make yourself strong as to make yourself miserable. It is in your power.

One technique I use on a daily basis that is making a positive difference is paying close attention to my thoughts. If I notice I am thinking in a negative way, ruminating over past events, or worrying about what people think of me, I say out loud my keyword 'Noise' and change my train of thought to something more productive. My psychiatrist recommended I try this idea, and it has served me well in my experiences.

Beliefs for promoting effective thinking:

- The situation doesn't do anything to me. I can react or not
- I don't need to take it personally
- Everything is exactly the way it is supposed to be
- We are all fallible human beings
- It takes two to have a conflict
- We feel the way we think

Running the Bipolar Marathon

Battling bipolar disorder is a lifelong war that can be compared to running a marathon. Marathon runners train, train, train, and then run the race to the best of their ability. Keep these steps in mind for running your personal bipolar marathon.

1. There are good days and bad days, and sometimes you can't tell the difference until you start.
2. Contrary to popular belief, sleep is not overrated—not in the slightest.

3. Don't forget to breathe.

4. Just because it's raining doesn't mean you should cry.

5. Nobody ever said it was easy.

6. Pain is temporary, but pride lasts a lifetime.

7. Create a plan and stick to it. It may not always work, but if you stay focused and relaxed, it will end up just fine.

8. You've got to try no matter what happens. In the end, you'll have biggest regrets from not trying at all.

9. Strength and courage blossom from the seeds of adversity.

10. Sometimes it's the little things that make the biggest differences.

11. Making it to the starting line is usually a lot harder than getting to the finish.

12. Listen to your body and listen to your mind. Make sure you acknowledge when they may be lying to you.

13. You can't change the past, and you won't alter the future. Enjoy your life in the present and always be positive!

14. Smile—it is contagious and increases endorphins. It actually takes more muscles and energy to frown.

15. It is okay to cry.

16. Don't forget to eat. Food can dictate your mood. If you take medication in the morning like I do, it is critical to eat to stabilize your sugar level and brain chemicals.

Notes

Notes

—Jean-Claude Van Damme, Actor

"God gave me a great body, and it's my duty to take care of my physical temple."

Diagnosed with Bipolar Disorder

Chapter 9
Train Your Body

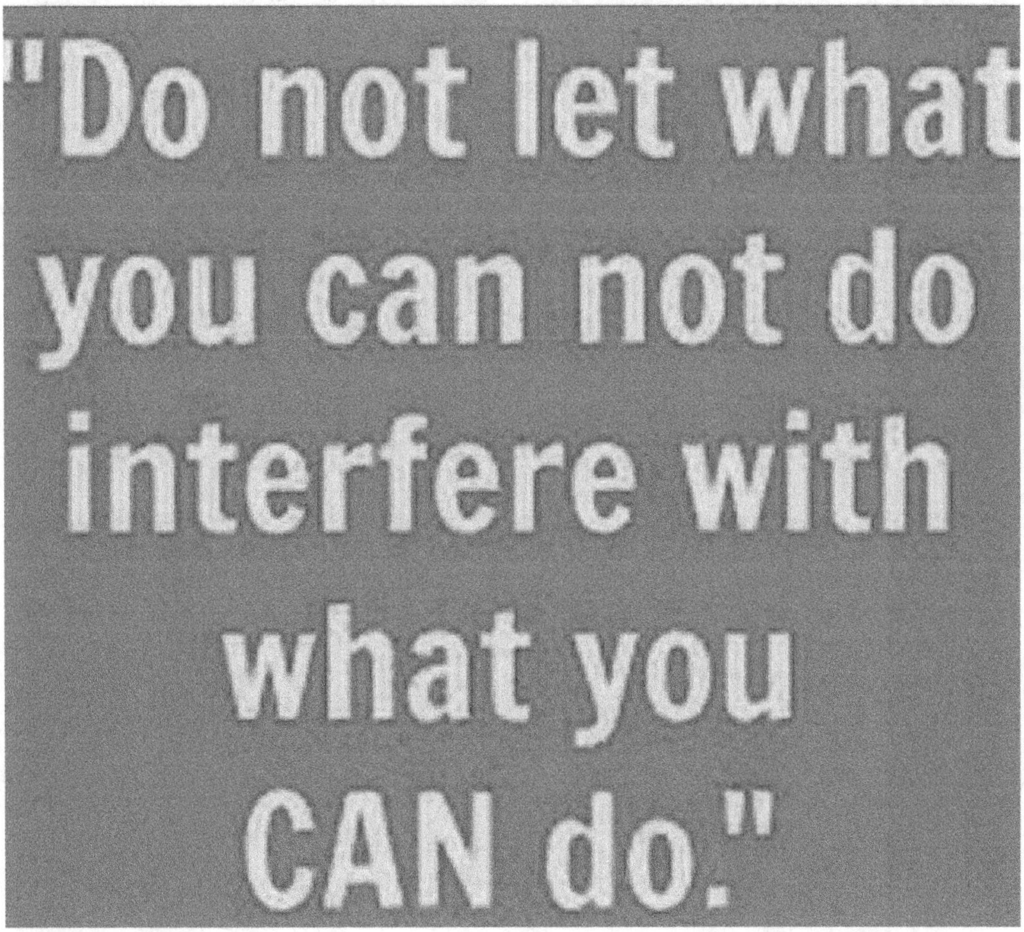

This chapter discusses:

- Healthy habits
- It is crucial to get enough sleep
- Stay away from sick people at all costs
- Stay hydrated

- Eat healthy
- Exercise
- Make Love
- Get fresh air and sunshine
- Drugs and alcohol

If you take care of your body, your body will in turn take care of you. Your mind and body are a unit; being good to your body benefits your mind. Taking care of your body will help stabilize your mood and maximize your energy for the battles ahead.

What you do to exercise your body is important, but what you don't do to your body is more important. By avoiding anything that is harmful, you will not obstruct the way your body naturally functions, and in return, your body will take care of you.

Healthy Habits
Fill in the prompts:

Healthy habits I practice regularly

____

Healthy habits I need to strengthen

____

New healthy habits I would like to develop

____

Healthy habits I used to have and would like to restart

____

Follow this list of actions to tune your body and improve your physical and mental health:

Train Your Body
Stay away from sick people at all costs
Eat healthy
Make love
Get fresh air and sunshine
Avoid drugs and alcohol
Shed extra pounds
Stretch your body every day
Take showers or baths
Animal Lovers

It is Crucial to Get Enough Sleep

For those of us who are bipolar it is **CRUCIAL** to get enough sleep. Lack of sleep is one of the strongest triggers of a bipolar episode. If you are having trouble sleeping, get a sleep aid from your psychiatrist. You can also try taking Melatonin or ZzzQuil if you want to try something over the counter. Meditation and herbal tea may also help.

Stay Away from Sick People at All Costs

I have an extreme phobia of being around people who are sick. If someone around you is sick (coughing, fever, etc.) or tells you they have recently been sick, immediately distance yourself from them. It may be necessary to make a scene, like moving to a new seat in a movie theater or at church. Just move away. I follow this rule whether I'm in line at the grocery, at the office, visiting my family, or anywhere else. Sometimes sick people will physically infringe on me, like coming into my cubicle at work to talk, attending a meeting I am at, or standing in close proximity to me. At times it seems like this person who is sick wants to get close to me so they can give away the illness. Don't let them infect you. Life is way too short to be sick, especially if you could have done something about it. Living with bipolar disorder is hard enough.

Sidenote written May 1, 2020:
[I wrote the paragraph above in December 2019, before the advent of the Corona Virus (COVID 19) pandemic spread across the globe. It has become more important than ever to heed this advice. In fact, it could be a matter of life or death. As of today's date, there have been 3,300,000 confirmed cases of COVID 19 worldwide, resulting in 235,000 deaths and 1,040,000 recoveries from the epidemic. The United States is the country which has been hit the hardest by COVID 19, with 1,130,000 confirmed cases resulting in 65,253 deaths and 137,000 recoveries. Scientists are scrambling to find a vaccine as the virus continues to wreak havoc around the world.]

Stay Hydrated

Pay attention to what your body is telling you—when you feel thirsty, replenish. It is important to flush your system and hydrate. In addition, fluids are very helpful when you are trying to lose weight because it reduces your appetite. Staying hydrated also helps your mind function more effectively.

Eat Healthy

Eat protein (steak, chicken, eggs and cheese), as well as salads, veggies, and fruit. Cut back on the bad carbohydrates (white bread, pasta, sweets). Good carbohydrates include rice, fruit, and potatoes. As with all things, balance is the key.

Make Love

Having sex with someone I like and who likes me back always energizes me and makes me feel better. I don't believe I am alone in these feelings. Intimacy as well as pleasure is good for us due to the dopamine released during sex. It is a natural 'high' that is your body's way of saying, "Thanks, I needed that!"

In his book, *Think and Grow Rich*, Napoleon Hill talks about the benefits of sex for maintaining good health:

"Sex desire is the most powerful of human emotions. For this very reason, the emotion of sex as a therapeutic agency for maintaining good health has no equal. The emotions are states of mind. When the emotion of love begins to mix itself with the emotion of sex, the result is calmness of purpose, poise, accuracy of judgement and balance. When love, romance, and sex are combined, these three emotions can lift one to the status of a genius."

Get Fresh Air and Sunshine

Getting fresh air every day clears your head, calms you down, and helps you appreciate the fact that you are alive on this awesome earth. Soak up the sun when you can. Looking directly at the sun with your eyes squinted just for a second or two is a way of gathering energy.

Stretch Your Body Every Day

Stretch your arms, legs, torso, and neck every day. Try to stay supple. This is especially important after sitting for extended periods of time.

Exercise

If you take care of your body, it will take care of you. Take walks, run, ride your bike, lift weights, dance, use the elliptical, do yoga, play basketball—do anything you enjoy that gets the blood pumping.

We are all different physically, and our energy levels vary from person to person. Start at whatever level you are now, and slowly increase your prowess. Build a strong core. In anatomy, the core refers to the body except for the legs and arms. The core is the power center. Besides the physical benefits, a strong core increases your willpower and sharpens your gut instincts. The core is one of the most important parts of the body to exercise and strengthen. Functional movements are highly dependent on the core, and lack of core development can result in a predisposition to injury. The major muscles of the core reside in the area of the belly, the middle and lower back, and peripherally the hips, the shoulders, and the neck.

You may find it easier to accomplish these actions if you incorporate them into your schedule on a consistent basis—for example, take walks every other day during your lunch break.

Drugs and Alcohol

More than 40 percent of us who are bipolar abuse alcohol or drugs, sometimes in an attempt to self-medicate. If you drink or do drugs, evaluate whether they are keeping you from being your best self. Also be mindful to consider whether you may be overdoing it to mask or numb your emotions. Drugs and alcohol can trigger an episode if you aren't careful, so treat them with respect.

I'm not preaching here. Believe me, I can relate. I used to smoke pot every day if I had a supply. My favorite brand was White Widow. When I was smoking, it was all or nothing. I used to tell myself I was a better man when I was stoned, with more energy and creativity, like Popeye eating spinach. However, after being in a couple of car wrecks because I was stoned out of my mind and realizing that weed was a contributing factor in my bipolar episodes, I admitted to myself that pot was more detrimental than beneficial for me. It wasn't easy to quit—marijuana is a powerful force. For several months after I quit smoking, I had dreams in which I was rolling joints from a large bag of Sensemilla containing huge, beautiful, moist, aromatic buds and then toking it up. Now that I have quit, I don't have the urge to smoke anymore. I can be around people who are smoking and I am not tempted. To to be clear, I am highly cognizant that if I get high even once I will be back to smoking every day, probably like people in AA know if they take one drink, they are going to get drunk, and getting back on the wagon is going to be difficult.

As I said, I have finally been able to stop smoking pot altogether. However, I still drink alcohol a couple of times a week. For now, this is the approach that is working for me. You will need to figure out what works best for you.

I like this passage found in the book *The Outsider* by Stephen King, which emphasizes the ritual casting off of bad habits and improving one's mental health:

"Holly paused, looking down at her hands. The nails were unpolished, but quite neat; she had quit chewing them, just as she had quit smoking. Broken herself of the habit. She sometimes thought that her pilgrimage to something at least approximating mental stability (if not genuine mental health) had been marked by the ritual casting off of bad habits. It had been hard to let them go. They were friends."

As an alternative to self-medicating with drugs and alcohol, learn to use bipolar medications to your advantage instead. Bipolar medications are very powerful pharmaceutical drugs and if used intelligently can work wonders.

Shed Extra Pounds

Losing weight is one of the hardest things to do. However, it is worth it. Your body functions better and your energy levels are higher when you aren't carrying too many extra pounds. As mentioned in the "Bipolar Disorder Facts and Statistics" section, approximately 25 percent of people with bipolar disorder are overweight, and sometimes obese. The good news is that being overweight can be controlled. By changing your diet, you can effectively lose weight and keep the pounds off.

My weight has fluctuated over the years. I will go on sprees in which I binge on barbecue chips, sweets, ice cream, and margaritas. Needless to say, I put on extra pounds during these times of lower will power, especially in the wintertime around the holidays. All of a sudden, I have gained 10 to 15 pounds and tend to start giving myself a hard time everyday until I gather enough willpower to begin dieting.

Be Patient and Give it Time.

When you begin losing weight, your motivation and sense of accomplishment will grow and make it easier to stick with the diet.

Maintaining your weight is a lifestyle change. Once you reach your target weight, be mindful that gaining weight is much easier and takes a lot less time than losing weight. If you stop watching what you eat, you will gain the weight back, and the sacrifice and extraordinary willpower you spent dieting will be for naught.

Get Your Thyroid Checked

Much of our day-to-day well-being: how energetic we feel, how clear our thinking is and how our body processes food, is governed by the activity of the butterfly-shaped, thumb-sized thyroid gland at the base of the throat. When it is working as it should, life is good. However, keep in mind that more than 12 percent of the U.S. population will develop a thyroid condition during their lifetime. The good news is that thyroid disease can be managed with medication.

Hypothyroidism (underactive thyroid) occurs when the thyroid gland does not produce enough hormones. If your thyroid hormone levels are too low, you may have fatigue, digestive problems, sensitivity to cold temperatures, and menstrual irregularities. If left untreated hypothyroidism can lead to many complications. These include heart problems, nerve injury, infertility and in severe cases, death.

Hyperthyroidism (overactive thyroid) occurs when your thyroid gland produces too much of the hormone thyroxine. Hyperthyroidism can accelerate your body's metabolism, causing unintentional weight loss and a rapid or irregular heartbeat.

Thyroid disease is associated with bipolar disorder and can actually cause bipolar symptoms as well as diabetes. Anyone who is bipolar should get their thyroid checked. There is a simple blood test that measures the amount of Thyroid Stimulating Hormone (TSH) in the body. Thyroid medicine can correct either a hypothyroid or hyperthyroid condition, both of which can mimic the symptoms of bipolar disorder.

Back in 2001, eight years after my first bipolar episode, my psychiatrist ordered a thyroid test as part of my regularly scheduled blood test to check my Lithium level. The results of the test showed that I have a hypothyroid condition, and I have been taking Levothyroxine on a daily basis ever since. I weighed 210 pounds at the time, and after being on thyroid medication for about four months, I was able to lose 30 pounds and I have pretty much maintained the same weight ever since. I attribute the weight loss to having a faster metabolism brought about by treating my hypothyroidism condition.

Note: Taking Lithium every day for a long time can cause thyroid problems as well as impact kidney function. If you take Lithium, then your doctor will have you take blood tests for Lithium levels and kidney functioning on a quarterly basis. I have been taking Lithium for over 20 years with no detrimental effect. In fact, if I had to choose one medication to take to treat my bipolar illness it would be Lithium because of the mood stability it manifests.

There are measures you can take to treat a thyroid condition, other than taking medication. Some of these include:

1. Keep up your mineral levels. The thyroid needs iodine to churn out hormones, and usually iodized salt or sea salt with natural iodine can supply most of our daily need of 150 micrograms.

2. Filter drinking water. Fluoride and chlorine are elements that can block the absorption of iodine into the thyroid.

3. Talk it out. In Eastern philosophy, the thyroid is located at the fifth chakra. This is the energy center of expression and communication. If you find yourself either regularly shouting or choking back your words, to support your thyroid on a deep emotional level, express yourself regularly to someone in your life such as a therapist, family member or good friend.

4. Make an appointment with an endocrinologist and get your thyroid checked out.

Take Showers or Baths

It is surprising how good it feels to take a shower or bath. Cleansing yourself with water relaxes you and makes you feel clean and refreshed. Take a long shower or bath to spend time focusing on yourself. Add candles, therapeutic salts, or your favorite music as enhancements. Just splashing cold water on your face is reviving.

Animal Lovers

Caring for an animal can provide companionship and be both therapeutic and rewarding. It is nice to have a feeling of being loved every time you come home. Unconditional love from a pal who needs you and always cares can be a key to maintaining consistent mental health. Another benefit is that you get more exercise, fresh air and sunshine when you take your dog on walks. It has been proven that petting a cat or dog can improve and enhance our mood.

Nasal Passage

One technique that I have used over the past several years is to frequently blow my nose throughout the day and keep my nasal passages clear. I haven't been sick since I implemented this method.

Brush your teeth and use mouthwash

To ward off disease and to feel better about yourself, brush your teeth regularly and use mouthwash.

Notes

—Carrie Fisher, Actress, Screenwriter

"I spent a year in a 12-step program, really committed, because I could not believe what had happened—that I might have killed myself."

Diagnosed with Bipolar Disorder

Chapter 10
Recovering from a Bipolar Episode

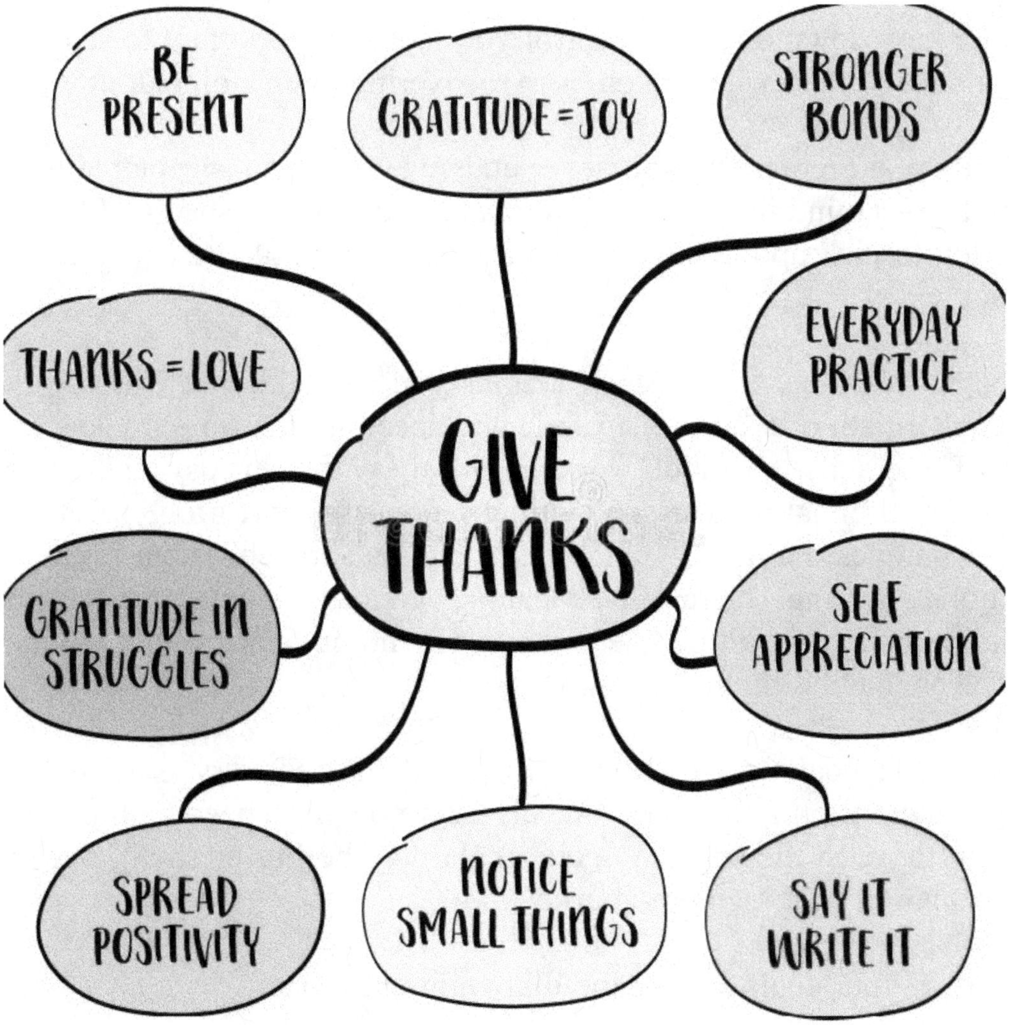

This chapter discusses:

- Physical symptoms of stress
- Practicing relaxation
- Promoting positive thinking
- Using coping techniques
- Ways therapy can help
- Things people do that do not aid in recovery

No matter how down or out of control you feel, it's important to remember that you are not powerless when it comes to recovering from a bipolar episode.

By definition, a bipolar episode never ends well since unacceptable things have happened, your mind has deceived you, and you have crashed and burned. Now you are left to pick up the pieces, regain your balance, and try to get back on an even keel.

This chapter provides a number of actions you can take that will help you deal with the aftermath of a bipolar episode and speed up the time it takes for you to recover. These actions include working closely with your psychiatrist regarding medications, eliminating stress, attending bipolar support group meetings, using coping techniques, forgiving yourself, setting goals, reaching out for face-to-face connections, getting therapy, educating yourself about bipolar disorder, surrounding yourself with people you can depend on, and making a plan to keep yourself from having future episodes.

Identifying life goals is the essential heart of the recovery process. When we identify and envision a future for ourselves, we begin to become motivated to do all we can to reach those goals. Your goals may be big or small, depending on where you are in your recovery journey.

When setting your goals answer the following questions:

Set Goals For Yourself
What motivates me?
What interests me?
What would I do more of if I could?
What do I want?
What did I care about before an episode?
Where do I want my life to go?
What brings me joy?
What are my hopes and dreams?
How am I going to make money to support myself?

Bipolar Support Groups:

I have attended Bipolar Support Group meetings in North Carolina, Connecticut and Florida and find them very helpful. I currently lead a bipolar support group meeting and am thankful for the opportunity.

The last thing I wanted to do after being released from the hospital was attend a support group. But after a few weeks of attending support group meetings, I realized that no matter how I felt before the meetings and no matter what was discussed during them, I always left feeling better.

The wonder of working with a collective group is that you get to learn from everyone within it. Often the best lessons can come from those who are struggling the most. Because I have had the chance to learn lessons vicariously through members of my support group, I have been able to avoid a great deal of suffering and heartache.

Do an online search to find a bipolar support group in your area, or an online support group.

Depression Bipolar Support Alliance:
https://www.dbsalliance.org/support/

The 7 Best Online Bipolar Disorder Support Groups:
https://www.verywellmind.com/best-online-bipolar-disorder-support-groups-4802211

Some of the things that helped me recover from my bipolar episodes that may help you also include:

Recovering From a Bipolar Episode
Work closely with your psychiatrist regarding medications
Eliminate stress
Attend support group meetings
Use coping techniques
Forgive yourself
Make a plan and set goals
Face to face connection
Get therapy
Educate yourself about Bipolar Disorder
Surround yourself with people you can depend on

Recovering From a Bipolar Episode
Have your own space
Understand recovery takes time
Contact your employer
Monitor your moods and symptoms
Get sunshine
Exercise
Don't abuse alcohol or drugs
Never quit. Make your dreams come true

BIPOLAR RECOVERY QUESTIONNAIRE

Use this questionnaire to determine if you are having manic or depressive symptoms and where you are in your recovery. Repeat it once a week to help you decide what course of action to take, i.e. make an appointment with your psychiatrist or therapist. Bring the answers with you to your appointment.

Mood & Symptom Assessment
Answer the questions using these criteria:

0 = Not at all   1 = Occasionally   2 = Often   3 = Very Often

Depressive Symptoms
Feeling sad or downhearted ________
Loss of interest or pleasure in activities ________
Changes in appetite or weight ________
Trouble sleeping or excessive sleeping ________
Fatigue or lack of energy ________
Feeling worthless or excessive guilt ________
Difficulty concentrating or making decisions ________
Thoughts of death or suicide ________

Manic/Hypomanic Symptoms
Elevated or irritable mood ________
Increased energy or restlessness ________
Decreased need for sleep ________
Racing thoughts or fast speech ________
Engaging in high-risk activities ________
Excessive involvement in pleasurable activities ________
Irritability or anger ________
Overconfidence or grandiosity ________

Use these checklists to ascertain the amount of stress in your life. Answer Yes or No.

Physical Symptoms of Stress		
	YES	NO
Heart pounding		
Headaches (steady pain)		
Neck, back or shoulder pain		
Frequent fatigue		
Muscle spasms		
Shortness of breath		
Asthma		
Excessive perspiration		
Overeating or lack of appetite		

Physical Symptoms of Stress		
	YES	NO
Difficulty sleeping		
Upset stomach		
Frequent colds / flu		
Lack of interest in sex		
Dry mouth		
Skin rash		

What happens when you practice relaxation?

What Happens When You Practice Relaxation?
Breathing slows down and deepens
Oxygen rate is lower
Heart rate decreases
Brain harmony is greater
Activity of key hormonal glands decreases
Feelings of well being increase
Greater physical balance
You will achieve positive changes in your life

Practicing deep relaxation even a few times a week can quickly help you restore greater balance in your body. And because body, mind, emotions, and spirit are all connected, you will experience positive changes in every area of your life.

Using positive thinking will help to reduce stress.

Beliefs for promoting positive thinking:

1. It (the situation) doesn't do anything to me. I can react or not.
2. I don't need to take it personally.
3. Everything is exactly the way it is supposed to be.
4. We are all fallible human beings.
5. It takes two to have a conflict.
6. We feel the way we think.

Use these simple 'thought changes' to change from negative thinking to positive thinking.

From awfulizing **. . . To a positive focus . . .**

- I'll NEVER get everything done!

  All the important things will get done. Slow down, breathe, and focus.

- I CAN'T stand waiting in lines.

  Waiting gives me a chance to practice my deep breathing, talk to someone new, or think about something fun.

- I REALLY messed up on that report. I AM a rotten person.

  That report could be improved. Who could I ask for input?

- If ONLY my boss, spouse or child would shape up, I wouldn't be so stressed.

  I am willing to give up the 'if only's.'

- I AM responsible for my own happiness.

  I can maintain my center even when things don't seem perfect!

Use Coping Techniques

There are many things you can do to reduce your symptoms and stay on track, including educating yourself about bipolar disorder, surrounding yourself with people you can count on, and leading a healthy 'wellness' lifestyle. With good coping skills and a solid support system, you can keep the symptoms of bipolar disorder in check, maintain your balance, and live fully and productively.

Here is a list of coping techniques that can be used to help you recover from a bipolar episode:

COPING SKILLS

***Identify triggers:**
-Look for triggers or circumstances that lead to feelings of despair
-Death or a Loss
-Alcohol use
-Stress from relationships

***Take care of yourself:**
-Eat healthy meals regularly
-Get plenty of rest and relaxation to help relieve stress
-Exercise is also important to help improve your emotional well-being

***Build a Support System:**
-Make the time to be around people with positive influences on your life and those who make you feel good about yourself
-Help others and giving back can be a great way to get out of your own head and to find meaning

***Get active:**
-Develop your own personal interests
-Find fun things to do
-Volunteer activities or work that give you a sense of purpose

***Relax:**
-Find personal ways to relieve stress levels
-Exercise
-Meditate
-Use sensory strategies to relax
-Practice simple breathing exercises
-Challenge your negative thoughts

Coping Techniques
Talk to a supportive person
Get a full 8 hours of sleep
Cut back on your activities
Attend a support group meeting
Meet with your psychiatrist and/or therapist
Do something fun and creative
Take time to relax and unwind
Increase your exposure to light
Exercise
Write in your journal

Coping Techniques
Eat healthy food
Drink lots of fluids
Avoid alcohol or drugs
Increase or decrease stimulation in your environment
Take adequate breaks of relaxation
Take a nature walk
Spend time with your loved ones
Take a bath
Take a nap

What Are Your Coping Resources?

Use the space below to answer the questions.

Who? Who can help you cope when you are having trouble doing things on your own?

____

What? What do you usually do when you absolutely must get something done even when you are not feeling up to it? What can you do to cope now?

____

Where? Where can you go for help if you are having trouble coping?

____

When? When is it easiest for you to cope when you are not feeling your best? Are you a morning person, or do you do your best work at night?

____

How? How can you make yourself cope when you are feeling stressed?

____

Therapy

While medication may be able to help you manage the symptoms of bipolar disorder, therapy teaches you skills you can use in all areas of your life and can be a powerful weapon on the road to full recovery. Therapy can help you learn how to deal with your illness, cope with problems, regulate your mood, change the way you think, and improve your relationships.

Therapy can teach you to:

Therapy Can Teach You To:
Understand your illness
Cope with stress
Make sense of post-traumatic experiences
Separate your personality from mood swings
Improve relationships with family and friends
Establish stable, dependable routines
Develop a plan for coping with crisis
Understand why things bother you and what you can do
End destructive habits like drinking and doing drugs

Dealing With the People Closest to You

While the things that you do and the way you behave during a bipolar episode vary widely in severity, they can sometimes be very disturbing, frightening, threatening, or intolerable. Sometimes sustaining a relationship with a significant other or family member is complicated due to financial insecurity, infidelity, alcoholism, addiction, abusiveness, criminal activity, or other factors that may be associated with the illness.

Things People Do That Do Not Aid in Your Recovery

Things People Do That Don't Aid In Your Recovery
Negative preaching or lecturing
Asking how you are doing too frequently
Watching and observing you all the time
Picking apart every thought and feeling you have
Checking if you are having symptoms too often
Trying to make you dependant on them
Not allowing you to handle situations on your own
Not respecting your independence

Maintaining emotional distance from a situation can be helpful.

WAYS TO GAIN EMOTIONAL DISTANCE
Walk Away From the Situation
Take Time to Evaluate the Situation
Ask Others Their Opinion of the Event
Sleep On It
Compare the Event to Other Experiences You Have Had
Ask Yourself How Others Might View What Happened
Watch Television
Change the Subject
Meditate
Take a Nap

Chapter Summary:

Recovering from a bipolar disorder involves a combination of structured routines, self-care practices, therapy, and active participation in treatment to stabilize mood and reduce episodes.

- Stick to a consistent routine – Daily Schedule stability
- Engage in regular exercise – Mood boosting activity
- Track mood patterns – Monitor emotional changes
- Build a strong support network – Reliable social connections
- Sleep hygiene – Consistent restful sleep
- Maintain a balanced diet – Nutrient-rich eating
- Limit stress with relaxation techniques – Mindful stress reduction
- Avoid alcohol and drugs – Substance-free lifestyle

Notes

Notes

—Jack Nicholson, Actor

"I know the voices aren't real, but man do they ever come up with some great ideas."

Played part of mental patient in movie "One Flew Over The Cuckoo's Nest"

Chapter 11
What You Need to Know About Psychiatric Hospitals

Hopefully you will never have to spend time in a psychiatric hospital. However, if you do, knowing what to expect is invaluable in speeding up your recovery and shortening your hospital stay.

This chapter discusses:

- Voluntary Check in
- Involuntary commitment
- Reasons to check into a psychiatric hospital
- Go with the flow
- Contacting your employer
- How hospitalization can help
- Don't leave the hospital too soon

Bipolar episodes can sometimes end with a stay in a psychiatric hospital, either by voluntarily checking yourself in or being involuntarily committed. Hopefully you will never need to go into the hospital. However, if you do, knowing what to expect is very helpful and can speed up the time it takes for you to recover.

It is an extremely hard decision to check yourself into a psychiatric hospital. However, when bipolar symptoms become severe and you are in the throes of a full-blown manic or depressive episode, checking yourself into the hospital can be the best possible move. Being in a psychiatric hospital is similar to being in any other hospital. You are there to heal, calm down, and be safe.

If you think you should check into a psychiatric hospital, do it before things go from bad to worse. Sometimes those of us with bipolar disorder need help and asking for it, although difficult, can help you avoid disaster. If you feel you do not have the strength to do it alone, find someone who supports you to take you to the hospital.

Get help so that you can live to fight another day. Dire consequences of not getting help can include suicide, self-mutilation, physical violence, or other catastrophic results. Recall that up to 20% of us end our lives by suicide, and 20-60% of us attempt suicide at least once in our lifetime.

Voluntary Check-In

Ways to check yourself into a psychiatric hospital include:

1. Go directly to a psychiatric hospital and tell them you need to be admitted. They will then ask you questions and based on your answers and the amount of available space, they may admit you or deny you. Most times, if you say you are suicidal at your evaluation, there is sufficient evidence for immediate admittance.

2. Work with your psychiatrist to be admitted.

3. Go to the emergency room of a hospital and tell them exactly what's going on and what you are thinking. They will transport you to a psychiatric hospital.

When you arrive at a psychiatric hospital, you will go to the Screening and Admissions Unit where you will be asked to sign a voluntary evaluation and admission form. Next, you will be examined by a hospital physician. If the physician agrees that you should be hospitalized, you will then be admitted.

Involuntary Commitment

Involuntary commitment is the act of placing someone into a psychiatric hospital or similar facility without their consent. Although such action may seem harsh, it is sometimes necessary in order to prevent people from harming themselves or others and to ensure that appropriate treatment is administered. Involuntary commitment is discussed in more detail in the following chapter.

Reasons to Check into a Psychiatric Hospital

- You are having thoughts of hurting yourself or others
- You are having hallucinations
- You feel unsafe, like you might lose control and start beating your head against the wall, jumping off of a bridge or some other dangerous act
- You are having bizarre or paranoid ideas (delusions)
- You have not eaten or slept for several days
- You have serious problems with alcohol or drugs
- You are thinking or talking too fast, jumping from topic to topic, or not making sense

- You feel too exhausted or too depressed to get out of bed or take care of yourself or your family

- You have tried outpatient treatment (therapy, medication, or support) and still have symptoms that interfere with your life

- You need to make a major change in your treatment or medication under the close supervision of your doctor

I have been in a psychiatric hospital three times due to bipolar episodes. I voluntarily checked myself in when I had my first episode in 1993 and then was involuntarily committed for my second major episode in 2005 and for my third major episode in 2012. The following is a list of things I learned along the way that can speed up your recovery if you find yourself in a psychiatric hospital.

Go with the Flow

An important thing to keep in mind when recovering from a bipolar episode in a psychiatric hospital is to go with the flow rather than trying to fight it. You should trust that the psychiatrist and the nursing staff who are treating you want you to get better and are trying to help. It is in your best interest to cooperate with them and take their advice. You will be in a structured environment where there are set rules to follow. You have set times to wake up and go to sleep, take medications, eat meals, attend group therapy, etc. The more you cooperate, the sooner you will begin to recover, and the sooner the psychiatrist will sign your discharge papers.

Contacting Your Employer from the Hospital

If you are in the hospital and you haven't let your boss know you will be missing work, when you feel up to it, tell the charge nurse you need to call your boss and they will facilitate the call. Decide how much you want to divulge—you don't necessarily have to say you are in a psychiatric hospital but saying you haven't been feeling yourself and you are in the hospital trying to find out what's wrong can be a valid excuse for missing work. Eventually you may have to own up that you are or were in a psychiatric hospital, but you can cross that bridge down the road. Once you make the phone call a huge weight will fall off your shoulders and you can then fully focus on your recovery.

How Hospitalization Can Help

Hospitalization can help in the following ways:

- The hospital is a safe place where you can begin to get well. It is a place to get away from the stresses that may be worsening your mood disorder and symptoms
- It's a private way to get help when you need it. You don't have to tell anyone from outside the hospital where you are, even your family, if you choose not to
- You can work with professionals to stabilize your severe symptoms, keep yourself safe, and learn new ways to cope with your illness
- You can talk about traumatic experiences and explore your thoughts, ideas, and feelings openly
- You can learn more about events, people, or situations that may trigger your manic or depressive episodes and how to cope with or avoid them
- You may find a new treatment or combination of treatments that work
- You will have time to reflect on your current situation and what improvements you can make

The Ins and Outs of Psychiatric Hospitals

Things to know if you are in a psychiatric hospital include:

- Whether you are a voluntary check-in or involuntary commitment, it is up to the psychiatrist treating you to decide when you can be discharged from the hospital. They must grant you permission to leave—you can't just check out
- You can make a reasonable number of phone calls

- You have the legal right to decide who can visit you and must sign a form giving them the right to do so

- Your medicine will be dispensed to you at set times, and a staff member will verify that you take the medicine

- You will have to follow a schedule. There will be set times for meals, treatments, medications, activities, and bedtime

- You may have physical or mental health tests. You may have blood tests to determine your medication levels or look for other physical problems that may be worsening your illness

- You might have to ask for things you need more than once

- Make sure that the doctor and the staff know about any other illnesses you have or medications you take. Be sure that you are receiving these medications

- Your prescribing doctor may not be able to see you right away. You will probably talk to several different doctors, nurses, and staff members

- You will meet other people who are working to overcome their own problems and interact with them. Treat them with courtesy and respect, regardless of what they may say or do. If someone is making you feel uncomfortable or unsafe, tell a staff member

- Some of the people you meet may be able to relate to you and understand what you are going through. It may be a way for you to build or strengthen your support group

- You may be in a locked ward. At first, you may not be able to leave the ward. Later, you may be able to go to other parts of the hospital or get a pass to leave the hospital for a short time

- You may have jewelry, personal care items, belts, shoelaces, or other personal belongings locked away during your stay. You may not be allowed to have items with glass or sharp edges, such as picture frames, CD cases, or spiral notebooks

- You may share a room with someone else

- In many places, the staff will not allow you to stay in your room for extended periods of time during the day. If you stay in your room, they may assume you are isolating yourself and keep you hospitalized until you can tolerate staying out in the common area with the other patients for a significant portion of the day for several days

- Hospital staff may check on you or interview you periodically

- After you begin to recover and heal, you may be able to request to transition from the hospital to an outpatient facility. This is a separate facility that lets you receive treatment during the day, sometimes in the morning or the afternoon, which allows you to be primarily at home and sleep in your own bed

Advice from Fellow Bipolar Warriors

Bipolar individuals who have been in a psychiatric hospital talk about their experiences and offer advice.

Gary:

"I was out of control, belligerent, and having hallucinations about being on a mission from God. I got in a fight in a bar with a bouncer who was giving me shit, and the cops came. I told them the bouncer was the devil. The police took me to a psychiatric hospital where I was involuntarily committed against my will. It took four days to heal up, but once I was back on my meds and had regained my balance, I told the doctor I had to get back to work, and he signed my discharge papers. The nurses and staff were very good to me, smiling and telling me to take it easy and things would improve. I'm not sure what would have happened if I had not ended up in the hospital."

Ruth:

"It is really useful to have a friend who understands you are bipolar and will help you out if you get into trouble. During an extremely bad episode, I was involuntarily committed into a psychiatric hospital. After several days of taking medication and 'coming to my senses,' I called my friend Joe and told him where I was and that I needed to get out of there and back to work. Joe drove to the hospital, talked to my doctor, and vouched for me. He told the doctor I was a sales manager and had a good job. The doctor discharged me and I will be eternally grateful to Joe because he had my back and helped me out in my time of need."

Scott:

"The benefits of being in the hospital for me include: You are in a controlled environment in the event of physical violence or attempted suicide. It gives you a chance to regroup and get stabilized. It removes you from stress of relationships—spouse, significant other, or kids. It is a forgivable excuse for missing work and may keep you from getting fired. The staff and doctors generally treat you well and take your craziness in stride. The food is usually decent. Finally, it's amazing how fast you can regain balance by taking medication."

Don't Leave the Hospital Too Soon

If you find yourself in a psychiatric hospital, give yourself time to begin the recovery process and get back on your feet again. Depending on how bad of shape you are in, it may be worthwhile to stay in the hospital a couple of days longer to regain balance, rather than trying to get out as soon as possible. Once you get back out in the real world there is a long road ahead to full recovery. When you get home from the hospital, some of the same things that were stressing you out and were instrumental in triggering your episode may still be present. These stressors could be a spouse, roommate, your children, bills, a sick relative or other factors.

Additional Recovery Tips

- Do what the doctor and nurses tell you to do
- Take the medications

- Eat the food they provide
- Sleep when you can
- Make friends with another patient
- Attend group therapy
- If possible, go outside and get fresh air and sunshine
- When it is offered, take a shower
- Brush your teeth
- Spend time in the common area instead of staying in your room most of the time—the nursing staff will be monitoring you, and staying isolated will extend your hospital stay
- There are usually several patients who are in bad shape and acting out. Try to avoid them

SUNSHINE
KINDNESS
SWEETS
cozy HOME
COFFEE
good MUSIC
THINGS TO BE grateful FOR:
PEACE
FLOWERS
CATS
FRIENDS and FAMILY
DOGS
road TRIPS
bike RIDES
CAMPING

Notes

—Terri Cheney, Lawyer, Writer

"Perilous highs and desperate lows and extravagant flurries of mood are not always symptoms of a broken mind, but signs of a beating heart."

Diagnosed with Bipolar Disorder

Chapter 12
Legal Rights

The information presented in this chapter is an overview of legal rights for the mentally ill based on material found on the internet. Legal rights for the mentally ill vary by state and by country. Always consult a lawyer who is well-versed in the laws where you live for legal advice.

This chapter discusses:

- Legal rights as an employee
- The American's. with Disabilities Act
- The laws governing involuntary commitment
- Legal rights as a patient in a psychiatric hospital
- Legal rights regarding medicine refusal
- The benefit of having a Psychiatric Advance Directive (PAD)
- Your legal rights for getting discharged from a Psychiatric hospital

Reference the following websites for detailed information about legal rights for the mentally ill:

https://mentalhealthrights.org/baker-act/

https://www.mhanational.org/issues/mental-health-rights

If you have bipolar disorder there are certain legal issues that may arise related to your condition, including job discrimination, consent to treatment issues, and trouble with the law.

Legal Rights as an Employee

One of the serious repercussions of having bipolar disorder is that you may miss work, sometimes days or even weeks at a time, especially if hospitalization occurs. It is important to know that if you have bipolar disorder, you often have disability rights with your employer, and you can take measures to protect your job. This includes many essential benefits, including health insurance. If you find yourself in this situation, talk to Human Resources at your work (discretely if possible) about your disability rights.

If the worst case happens and you become unemployed, you may still have rights with your employer. Consult a lawyer who specializes in employment law to find out if you have any recourse.

The Americans with Disabilities Act

The Americans with Disabilities Act (ADA) is a law that gives civil rights protection to individuals with disabilities. The ADA's legal definition of a disability is especially beneficial to those with bipolar disorder. According to the US Equal Employment Opportunity Commission, the ADA defines the term disability as "a physical or mental impairment that substantially limits a major life activity." Since bipolar disorder seriously affects people's ability to work, the ADA is of vital importance to those with the disorder. It ensures that people with bipolar disorder have rights at work and, in serious cases provides them with disability benefits if they are unable to work due to their condition.

I was employed by different employers during two of my bipolar episodes, both of which involved me being hospitalized in a psychiatric hospital. I was fortunate in both cases. Once I came to my senses, I called my boss from the hospital and told him where I was and that I would get back to work as soon as I could. In each case my supervisor got Human Resources involved and I was thankfully able to keep my job.

To find out more about the ADA, consult the following website:

https://www.ada.gov/

The Laws Governing Involuntary Commitment

Involuntary commitment is a legal process through which an individual with symptoms of severe mental illness is court-ordered into a psychiatric hospital against their will. In general, laws restrict involuntary commitment to those who are 'mentally ill' and/or under the influence of drugs or alcohol and are deemed to be in imminent danger of harming themselves or others.

If the police are called to a location, for whatever reason, and observe that you are suicidal, belligerent, threatening, or physically violent, they may take you to a psychiatric hospital or they may take you to jail. The immediate safety of you and anyone else is the primary concern. If you are bipolar, you should be taken to a psychiatric hospital for evaluation instead of a jail cell. However, many times the police won't realize you are bipolar. If you end up in jail due to a bipolar episode, tell the police and your lawyer that you are bipolar. You do have rights!

Reasons you can be involuntarily committed to a psychiatric hospital include:

1. You attempt suicide or attempt to harm yourself.

2. Many of us who are bipolar have a history of explosive behavior. Some may call this rage, mania, violence, or anger. If you become aggressive or violent with others you can be involuntarily committed to a psychiatric hospital.

3. A family member or someone else has you committed.

With most adverse bipolar behavior, those most affected are usually the people who are closest to the bipolar individual, such as family or friends. If you are having a bipolar episode and are violent, suicidal, or making threats, a family member or someone else may decide to take action and have you committed to a psychiatric hospital.

At the time, it will most likely seem harsh. These types of cases of involuntary committal are usually accompanied by strong emotions of the person committed and the person responsible for the committing. It is highly possible that this person is taking this action because they want to keep you, themselves or others safe until the episode runs its course.

If someone is attempting to have you committed to a psychiatric hospital against your will, get a lawyer. Bipolar episodes are scary, confusing, and heart wrenching. It is to your advantage to consult with someone who is not emotionally involved to steer you through the legal issues and protect your legal rights.

In the rare case that the person who is attempting to have you involuntarily committed is trying to do you harm rather than help you, keep your wits about you as much as possible and, again, get a lawyer. Maybe you have not been getting along with that person and he or she is on the warpath against you. Do your best to remain calm and collected when you come before the judge and convince them that there is no reason for you to be hospitalized. Explain that the person is making false accusations. Your psychiatrist can be your best advocate in court.

Someone who decides to have you involuntarily committed to a psychiatric hospital must take the following steps:

1. They will file an affidavit with the clerk of superior court or magistrate of district court. The clerk or magistrate may issue an order to a law enforcement officer to take you into custody for examination by a qualified professional.

2. If the qualified professional finds that you are 'mentally ill,' you will most likely be taken to a psychiatric hospital.

3. When you arrive at the hospital you will be examined by a psychiatrist. If the hospital psychiatrist agrees with the first examiner that hospitalization is necessary, you will be admitted for observation and treatment. If they do not believe you should be in the hospital, you will be released.

4. A court hearing must be held no later than ten days after you are taken into custody. The hearing may be held either in the county where the commitment was initiated or at the hospital. Within a few days after you are admitted, a lawyer from the Office of Special Counsel will contact you. They will be your lawyer at the initial hearing. You may also hire a lawyer at your own expense. At the hearing, the judge will decide whether you should be treated in the hospital or discharged. If you are committed, the judge will decide how many days you will be kept in the hospital before another hearing must be held.

At the hearing, you have the following rights:

- The right to an attorney (you may hire your own, or an attorney can be provided for you)

- The right to be present at the hearing

- The right to speak for yourself
- The right to challenge what is said about you

Legal Rights as a Patient in a Psychiatric Hospital

If you find yourself in a psychiatric hospital you have the following legal rights:

- It is your legal right that the hospital staff verbally explains and provides you with a written copy of the privacy policy, which gives you the right to choose whether you want to have visitors or not. Staff will get a list from you of people you agree can visit you. If you do not wish to have outside friends, family members, employers, or anyone else know you're there, the staff will not make your presence known. They cannot legally verify in any way that you are a patient
- You may immediately make telephone calls in order to get help with legal, medical, and mental health issues
- You have the right to be visited by your clergy, lawyer, or physician at any time, within visiting hours
- You have the right to ask for help from hospital staff to make sure your rights are honored
- You have the right to a civil commitment hearing where a judge will decide whether you should be hospitalized by court order. You have the right to a court-appointed attorney at the court hearing. It is highly recommended to have a lawyer represent you at a court hearing to protect your legal rights
- You have the right to an independent expert evaluation of your mental condition. If you cannot afford this evaluation, it must be provided to you at no charge

- You have the right to file a grievance with the hospital if you feel your rights have been violated. You can request the hospital's clients' rights officer to help you with filing your grievance

- You may communicate by sealed mail with any individual, group, or agency

- You have the right to be furnished with writing materials and reasonable postage

- You have the right to receive mail, unless the head of the hospital determines it is medically harmful for you to receive mail

- You have the right to receive visitors at regular hours, unless the head of the hospital determines it is medically harmful for you to receive visitors. The people who want to visit you must be notified immediately when you have recovered sufficiently to receive visitors

- You have the right to wear your own clothes

- You have the right to keep and use personal possessions (excluding anything deemed potentially harmful), including toiletries

- You have the right to request to be released from the hospital

Legal Rights Regarding Medication Refusal

The standard procedure for dealing with medication refusal is to take the patient to court to legally force he or she to agree to take it. At the trial, the psychiatrist will explain exactly why they think you need to be hospitalized and why it is important for you to take medication. The judge then rules that you either have to take medication or don't have to take it. If so, this means that even if you refuse medication, you are legally obligated to take it. When you return to the psychiatric hospital, the doctors will offer you oral meds first, but if you will not take them, staff members will physically restrain you and administer the medication.

The Benefits of Having a Psychiatric Advance Directive (PAD)

In order to protect yourself when you are experiencing a bipolar episode it is to your benefit to prepare a Psychiatric Advance Directive (PAD) in advance.

The PAD is a legal contract that allows you to choose and control in advance the care you will receive when you are mentally incapacitated and are unable to direct your own care during potential times of crisis. It serves to inform others about what treatment you do want or don't desire from psychiatrists or other mental health professionals in the event of a bipolar episode.

A PAD allows you to identify a person to whom you have given authority to make decisions on your behalf. Instead of having some stranger make the decisions or have your family guess at what you would want, you can list your preferences.

Almost all states permit some form of legal Advance Directive. Google a PAD for your state. Here are four websites about making a PAD:

https://documentify.com/generate-advance-directive?msclkid=51c0f6e0a7601c7bd5e39ccd3c4ace21

https://rightsandrecovery.org/wp-content/uploads/2025/09/Psychiatric-Advanced-Directive-PAD-Toolkit.pdf

National Resource Center on Psychiatric Advance Directives:
www.nrc-pad.org

National Alliance On Mental Health (NAMI) Psychiatric Advance Directives (PAD):

https://www.nami.org/Advocacy/Policy-Priorities/Improve-Care/Psychiatric-Advance-Directives-(PAD)

Typical provisions in a Psychiatric Advancer Directive include the following:

What To Include in a Psychiatric Advance Directive
Person you want to take care of your children
Medication instructions
Choice of hospital
List of emergency contacts
The following may cause me to have a Bipolar Episode
The following may help me avoid a Bipolar Episode
List of people who can visit you in the hospital
What you want to be taken care of in your home
Preferences as to whether you agree to special therapies

Your Legal rights for Getting Discharged from a Psychiatric Hospital

There is a process that must be followed for getting discharged from a psychiatric hospital. If you decide you want to be discharged, you cannot simply sign yourself out and leave when you decide to do so. You can request to be discharged by filling out the correct paperwork. If the request for discharge is approved, you will be allowed to leave within three workdays (Monday through Friday, not weekends or holidays). If you request to be discharged, there are three possible outcomes:

- The psychiatrist who is handling your case will agree that you can leave. When your request to be discharged is granted, you can leave at the end of seventy-two hours

- There are cases in which someone who admitted themselves voluntarily to the psychiatric hospital is not allowed to leave of their own accord because the doctors and staff feel they are harmful to themselves or others. In this case, the hospital staff can ask the court to commit you. The hospital staff must file papers (an affidavit) within three workdays of receiving your 'request of discharge' form. Your request for release becomes a request for a hearing. You will receive notice of a court hearing before a judge to determine whether a court order will be issued to keep you in the hospital. At the hearing, if the judge rules that you need to stay in the hospital you become an involuntary patient; otherwise you will be discharged

- If the hospital does not file an affidavit within three workdays, you must be released immediately

Notes

—Mariah Carey, Singer, Songwriter

"I think it's completely reasonable to feel like you're unwilling to face your diagnosis in the beginning. What's important is that you keep trying, day by day."

Diagnosed with Bipolar Disorder

Chapter 13
Winning the Bipolar War

Here we are full circle. I hope you have a better understanding of Bipolar Disorder and now have a plan to follow in the future to remain episode free. My Bipolar Battle Plan has been working for me for over ten years although I am cognizant if I don't follow the plan, I may very well become manic or depressed.

Remember, Bipolar Disorder is treatable. Controlling the symptoms of bipolar disorder is an ongoing process. You must be relentless about getting necessary treatment and sticking to it. This book has instructed you how to create a bipolar battle plan that can help you learn to cope with your emotions, control negative thinking, minimize physical symptoms, deal with medication issues, manage problems within everyday life, and effectively treat your illness.

Remember that in war all battle plans can be altered. Be prepared to make changes to your plan when you find it necessary to do so. Change your plan as many times as needed until you achieve optimal mental and physical health.

Make the commitment to become a warrior, master the weapons in your bipolar battle plan, and win the war against bipolar disorder. Winning the war means never having another out-of-control bipolar episode that causes you to attempt suicide, harm yourself or others, end up in the psychiatric hospital, wreck your finances, lose your job, destroy relationships with friends and loved ones, or destroy your health. Winning the war means living a productive, happy life and making your dreams come true!

Remember *Bipolar Heal Thyself.*

Bipolar Battle Plan Summary

Bipolar Battle Plan Summary
Bipolar Heal Thyself - take responsibility for your own treatment
Adopt the mindset of a warrior every day
Create your own personal Bipolar Battle Plan
Take action every day to further your plan
Monitor your moods (emotions and feelings)
Be vigilant for Bipolar symptoms
Create a support team and use them
Launch your Contingency Plan if needed
Optimize your medications
Watch out for side effects

Bipolar Battle Plan Summary
Find a good psychiatrist
Never stop learning about the enemy Bipolar Disorder
Train and strengthen your mind
Train and strengthen your body
Monitor your thoughts. Deny negativity
Don't abuse drugs and alcohol
Never quit. Make your dreams come true

YOU HAVE ALL THE WEAPONS YOU NEED—NOW FIGHT!

Notes

If you find this workbook useful, please take a few moments to write a review on your favorite store, and please refer it to anyone you know who you think may benefit from it.

You could be saving their life!

I wish you the very best!

Thanks, Troy

Additional Books by Troy Steven:

Amazon Link: https://www.amazon.com/dp/1513650440

Amazon Link: https://www.amazon.com/dp/B0BCD5C7BL

Amazon Link: https://www.amazon.com/dp/B0BCD5C7BL

Appendix A: DBSA Wellness Wheel

DBSA WELLNESS WHEEL:

The Depression and Bipolar Support Alliance (DBSA) is the leading national organization focused on depression and bipolar disorder. DBSA provides peer-led support, trusted resources, and wellness tools for individuals living with mood disorders – as well as for their family members, friends, parents, and caregivers. They provide a tool called the DBSA Wellness Wheel that can be used to take an inventory of your strengths in 7 key areas:

Physical Wellness:

Involves taking steps to find healthy habits that can support overall wellness and focuses on nutrition, exercise and sleep.

Occupational Wellness:

Involves finding work that is satisfying and aligns with personal values and goals. Wellness in this area is also about balancing work with personal life and leisure time.

Financial Wellness:

Involves learning how to manage expenses. Wellness in this area also means considering spending and saving habits.

Environmental Wellness:

Involves living in harmony with both natural and built spaces. Wellness in this area means enjoying your surroundings, modifying them to suit you, and caring for the earth.

Social Wellness:

Involves creating and sustaining healthy, supportive relationships. Wellness in this area means considering how to connect with others and create community.

Intellectual Wellness:

Involves participating in activities that increase curiosity. Wellness in this area involves considering how having hobbies and interests can continue to stimulate our passions.

Spiritual Wellness:

Involves finding connection with values, meaning and purpose. Wellness in this area includes practices that can create connection with community and our higher selves.

You can find the forms to complete the Wellness Wheel here:

https://www.dbsalliance.org/wellness/wellness-toolbox/dbsa-wellness-wheel/

Appendix B: Therapeutic & Clinical Tools

- **Psychotherapy**: CBT (Cognitive Behavioral Therapy) for thought patterns, IPSRT (Interpersonal & Social Rhythm Therapy) for routines, Family-Focused Therapy for support

- **Medication** Management: Mood stabilizers, antipsychotics; apps like Medisafe help track adherence

- **Psychoeducation**: Learning about bipolar disorder helps you and your family manage it

- **Clinical Scales:** Tools like the YMRS or Mood Disorder Questionnaire (MDQ) for tracking symptom severity

Self-Management & Digital Tools:

- **Mood & Symptom Trackers**: Apps like eMoods, PolarUs, and MoodTrack Diary help log highs/lows, sleep, and triggers

- **Routine & Sleep Apps**: Consistency in sleep/eating is crucial; apps help maintain this

- **Mindfulness & Relaxation Apps** like Calm offer guided meditation, breathing exercises, and sleep stories

- **Resource Hubs**: CREST.BD provides quality of life tools and self-management strategies

Lifestyle & Support:

- **Consistent Routine:** Stable sleep, diet, and exercise times are vital
- **Support Groups** Connecting with others facing similar challenges
- **Light Therapy:** Can help those affected by seasonal changes

Professional Treatment:

- **Medication**:

  Mood stabilizers (lithium, valproate, lamotrigine), antipsychotics (quetiapine, aripiprazole), and sometimes antidepressants (with mood stabilizers) are used to regulate extreme highs (mania/hypomania) and lows (depression)

- **Psychotherapy** (Talk Therapy):

  - **CBT (Cognitive Behavioral Therapy)**: Changes negative thought/behavior patterns
  - **DBT (Dialectical Behavior Therapy)**: Helps with emotional regulation and impulse control
  - **Interpersonal & Social Rhythm Therapy** (IPSRT): Stabilizes daily routines (sleep, eating, socializing) to prevent mood shifts
  - **Family-Focused Therapy (FFT):** Educates and involves family in managing the disorder

Self-Care & Lifestyle:

- Routine: Maintain regular sleep, eating, and activity schedules to stabilize moods
- Stress Reduction: Practice mindfulness, yoga, deep breathing, and ensure proper nutrition and exercise
- Support: Join support groups (like DBSA) or build new relationships to combat isolation

For Loved Ones:

- Offer patience, understanding, and emotional support
- Help with practical tasks like appointments
- Learn triggers and recognize mood changes.

Immediate Help:

- If you or someone you know is having suicidal thoughts, call or text the 988 Suicide & Crisis Lifeline

Appendix C: Resources

Americans with Disabilities Act (ADA) - a law that gives civil rights protection to individuals with disabilities:
https://www.ada.gov/

Area of brain linked to bipolar disorder pinpointed. Article in Science Daily discussing which areas of the brain are affected by bipolar disorder and their specific impact:
https://www.sciencedaily.com/releases/2017/01/170124144000.htm

Black Dog Institute: An educational, research, and clinical facility offering specialized expertise in mood disorders:
www.blackdoginstitute.org.au

BP Magazine: An excellent quarterly magazine about bipolar disorder that also comes in an online version and has a great online forum, making it easy to ask questions and get answers:
http://www.bphope.com

Depression and Bipolar Support Alliance
https://www.dbsalliance.org/support/

GoodRx. Prescription Discount Site:
www.goodrx.com

MHA. Mental Health America.
https://www.mhanational.org/issues/mental-health-rights

MHR. Mental Health Rights:
https://mentalhealthrights.org/baker-act/

National Institute of Mental Health (NIMH): The mission of the NIMH is to transform the understanding and treatment of mental illness through basic and clinical research, paving the way for prevention, recovery, and cure:
http://www.nimh.nih.gov/index.shtml

NeuroStar TMS: Transcranial magnetic stimulation therapy is an FDA-cleared non-invasive medical treatment that is specifically for patients with major depression who have not benefited from initial antidepressant medication:
http://neurostar.com/nondrug-treatment-for-depression/?gclid=CNa_na6hi7QCFQf0nAodBigAoA

http://www.youtube.com/NeurostarTMSTherapy

Newharbinger Publications: Excellent source on Mood Disorders:
http://www.newharbinger.com

Non-Medical Treatment for Bipolar Disorder:
http://www.ehow.com/facts_5685287_non_medical-treatment-bipolar-disorder.html#ixzz1xPMeZGdE

Psychiatric Advanced Directive (PAD) Explanation:
https://www.nami.org/Advocacy/Policy-Priorities/Improve-Care/Psychiatric-Advance-Directives-(PAD)

Psychiatric Advance Director – Download Your State's Advance Directive Form:
https://www.nhpco.org/patients-and-caregivers/advance-care-planning/advance-directives/downloading-your-states-advance-directive

The Best Bipolar Disorder Apps for 2019 can be found at the following website:
https://www.healthline.com/health/bipolar-disorder/top-iphone-android-apps#imoodjournal

The 7 Best Online Bipolar Disorder Support Groups of 2020:
https://www.verywellmind.com/best-online-bipolar-disorder-support-groups-4802211

Wikipedia is a free online encyclopedia with an excellent overview and description of bipolar disorder:
http://en.wikipedia.org/wiki/Bipolar_disorder

Appendix D: Bibliography

Alloy, Lauren. 2017. "Circadian Rhythm Dysregulation in Bipolar Spectrum Disorders." Accessed June 4, 2019. https://www.ncbi.nlm.nih.gov/pmc/articles/PMC6661150/

American Thyroid Association. 2020. "Prevalence and Impact of Thyroid Disease." Accessed January 15, 2020. https://www.thyroid.org/media-main/press-room/#:~:text=An%20estimated

Bailey, Eileen. 2019. "9 Famous People With Bipolar." Accessed May 15, 2020. https://www.healthcentral.com/slideshow/6-famous-people-bipolar-disorder

Bhandari, Smitha. 2019. "Celebrities With Bipolar Disorder." Accessed May 1, 2020. https://www.webmd.com/bipolar-disorder/ss/slideshow-celebrities-bipolar-disorder

Bhatia, Juhie. 2018. "13 Famous People With Bipolar Disorder." Accessed May 15, 2020. https://www.everydayhealth.com/bipolar-disorder-pictures/famous-people-with-bipolar-disorder.aspx

Bledsoe, Andrea. 2010. "Bipolar Disorder and Migraines." Accessed December 6, 2019. https://www.everydayhealth.com/hs/bipolar-depression/bipolar-disorder-and-migraines/
Bocchetta, Alberto. 2016. "Bipolar disorder and anti-thyroid antibodies: review and case series". Accessed June 5, 2019. https://journalbipolardisorders.springeropen.com/articles/10.1186/s40345-016-0046-4

Bowden, Charles. 2005. "Bipolar Disorder and Work Loss." Accessed January 2, 2019. https://journalbipolardisorders.springeropen.com/articles/10.1186/s40345-016-0046-4

Bressert, Steve. 2020. "Causes of Bipolar Disorder." Accessed March 5, 2020. https://psychcentral.com/bipolar/bipolar-disorder-causes/

Burgess, Lana. 2016. "What is psychomotor agitation?" Accessed April 2, 2020. https://www.medicalnewstoday.com/articles/319711

Burgess, Lana. 2019. "Is there a cure for Bipolar Disorder?" Accessed September 25, 2019. https://www.medicalnewstoday.com/articles/324349.php

Carlos Castaneda's Don Juan Teachings. Accessed June 6, 2013. http://www.prismagems.com/castaneda/donjuan8.html

Castaneda, Carlos. 1998. The Wheel of Time. New York: Pocketbooks.

Cerullo, Michael. 2007. "The prevalence and significance of substance use disorders in bipolar I and II disorder." Accessed January 6, 2020. https://www.ncbi.nlm.nih.gov/pmc/articles/PMC2094705/

Chakrabarti, Subho. 2011. "Thyroid Functions and Bipolar Affective Disorder." Accessed December 1, 2019. https://www.ncbi.nlm.nih.gov/pmc/articles/PMC3144691/

Chugani, Harry. 1987. "Positron emission tomography study of human brain functional development." Accessed December 5, 2019. https://onlinelibrary.wiley.com/doi/abs/10.1002/ana.410220408

Cirino, Erica. 2019. "Can You Have Bipolar Disorder and an Anxiety Disorder at the Same Time?" Accessed February 8, 2020. https://www.healthline.com/health/bipolar-and-anxiety

Citizens Commission On Human Rights. 2020. "Mental Health Declaration of Human Rights." Accessed March 5, 2020. https://www.cchr.org/about-us/mental-health-declaration-of-human-rights.html

Clark, Luke. 2008. "Cognitive neuroscience and brain imaging in bipolar disorder." Accessed June 6, 2019. https://www.ncbi.nlm.nih.gov/pmc/articles/PMC3181872/

Connell, Kelly. 2019. "Bipolar Disorder and Sexual Health." Accessed February 10, 2020. https://www.healthline.com/health/bipolar-disorder/guide-sexual-health

Cooney, Lewis. 2017. "Overview of systematic reviews of therapeutic ranges: methodologies and recommendations for practice." Accessed June 6, 1019. https://bmcmedresmethodol.biomedcentral.com/articles/10.1186/s12874-017-0363-z

Cronkleton, Emily. 2019. "Why Is Vitamin B Complex Important, and Where Do I Get It?" Accessed June 6, 2019. https://www.healthline.com/health/food-nutrition/vitamin-b-complex

Dome, Peter. 2019. "Suicide Risk in Bipolar Disorder: A Brief Review." Accessed January 6, 2020. https://www.ncbi.nlm.nih.gov/pmc/articles/PMC6723289/

Dutta, Sanchari. 2019. "What is Norepinephrine?" Accessed January 3, 2020. https://www.news-medical.net/health/What-is-Norepinephrine.aspx

Feather, Ken. 1995. On The Toltec Path. VT: Bear & Company.

Foundations Recovery Network. 2020. "Untreated Bipolar Disorder Can Lead to Increased Risk of Domestic Violence." Accessed January 3, 2020. https://dualdiagnosis.org/bipolar-disorder-and-addiction/domestic-violence-and-bipolar-disorder/#:~:text=a%20Manic%20Episode-,Bipolar%20Disorder%20and%20Domestic%20Violence,to%20the%20bipolar%20person's%20partner

Ghaemi, Nassir. 2011. "Positive Aspects of Mental Illness: A Review on Bipolar Disorder." Accessed March 5, 2013. http://www.bphope.com/item.aspx/915/accentuate-the-positive

Gibbons-Gwyn, Malinda. 2009. "Bipolar Disorder and Decision Making." Accessed February 9, 2020. https://www.everydayhealth.com/bipolar-disorder/bipolar-disorder-and-decision-making.aspx#:~:text=Bipolar%20Disorder-,Bipolar%20Disorder%20and%20Decision%20Making,responsibility%20and%20manage%20your%20emotions.&text=The%20dramatic%20mood%20swings%20of,particularly%20during%20a%20manic%20episode.

Hage, Mirella. 2011. "Thyroid Disorders and Diabetes Mellitus." Accessed June 5, 2019. https://www.ncbi.nlm.nih.gov/pmc/articles/PMC3139205/#:~:text=Studies%20have%20found%20that%20diabetes,management%20of%20diabetes%20in%20patients

Harvey, Allison. 2015. "Interventions for Sleep Disturbance in Bipolar Disorder." Accessed December 2, 2019. https://www.ncbi.nlm.nih.gov/pmc/articles/PMC4347516/

Haycock, Dean. 2010. "The Everything Health Guide to Adult Bipolar Disorder." MA: Adams Media.

Healthessentials. 2020. "Why Having a Pet Can Boost Your Mood and Keep Your Brain Healthy." Accessed May 1, 2020. https://health.clevelandclinic.org/why-having-a-pet-of-any-kind-may-boost-your-mood-and-keep-your-brain-healthy/

HelpGuide. 2020. "Bipolar Disorder Signs and Symptoms." Accessed January 29, 2020. https://www.helpguide.org/articles/bipolar-disorder/bipolar-disorder-signs-and-symptoms.htm
HelpGuide. 2020. "Bipolar Disorder Treatment." Accessed February 7, 2020.

https://www.helpguide.org/articles/bipolar-disorder/bipolar-disorder-treatment.htm

Hibar, D. 2017. "Bipolar disorder affects brain regions controlling inhibition, emotion." Accessed June 6, 2019.
https://www.healio.com/news/psychiatry/20170605/bipolar-disorder-affects-brain-regions-controlling-inhibition-emotion

Hill, Napoleon. 1997. Napoleon Hill's Keys to Success. New York: Plume.

Hill, Napoleon 2012. Think and Grow Rich. Aristeus-Books.

Hook, Debra-Lynn. 2015. "How Seasonal Pattern Affects Bipolar Disorder." Accessed May 1, 2020.
https://www.everydayhealth.com/depression/seasonal-depression-and-bipolar.aspx

Hornbacher, Marya. 2008. Madness: A Bipolar Life. New York: First Mariner Books.

Huizen, Jennifer. 2019. "Medications for bipolar disorder: What you should know." Accessed January 3. 2020.
https://www.medicalnewstoday.com/articles/324388

Jamison, Kay. 1996. An Unquiet Mind. New York: First Vintage Books.

Jamison, Kay. 1994. Touched with Fire. New York: Free Press Paperbacks.

Kessler, R. C. 2005. "The Numbers Count: Mental Disorders in America." Accessed March 10, 2013.
https://www.nimh.nih.gov/health/statistics/index.shtml

Kildare, Sasha. 2020. "The Essential Guide To Maintaining Friendships With Bipolar." Accessed March 6, 2020.
https://www.bphope.com/friendships-bipolar-maintaining/

King, Stephen. 2018. The Outsider. New York: Simon & Shuster, Inc.

Krans, Brian. 2017. "Diagnosis Guide for Bipolar Disorder." Accessed September 25, 2019.
https://www.healthline.com/health/bipolar-disorder/bipolar-diagnosis-guide

Kvarnstorm, Elisabet. 2018. "Understanding Bipolar Disorder Triggers and How to Prevent Them." Accessed December 2, 2019.
https://www.bridgestorecovery.com/blog/understanding-bipolar-disorder-triggers-and-how-to-prevent-them/
Leech, Joe. 2018. "11 Proven Health Benefits of Garlic". Accessed June 3, 2019.

https://www.healthline.com/nutrition/11-proven-health-benefits-of-garlic#section1

Leech, Joe. 2018. "10 Evidence-Based Health Benefits of Cinnamon." Accessed June 3, 2019. https://www.healthline.com/nutrition/10-proven-benefits-of-cinnamon#section10

Legg, Timothy. 2019. "Energy level Combatting Bipolar Disorder Related Fatigue." Accessed February 5, 2020.
https://www.healthline.com/health/bipolar-disorder/guide-fatigue#sleep-smarter

Legg, Timothy. 2020. "What Causes Bipolar Disorder?" Accessed May 9, 2020. https://www.healthline.com/health/bipolar-disorder/bipolar-causes

Legg, Timothy. 2019. "What Does It Mean to Have a Parent with Bipolar Disorder?" Accessed January 3, 2019.
https://www.healthline.com/health/bipolar-disorder/how-to-deal-with-a-bipolar-parent

Leonard, Jayne. 2019. "Bipolar Type Definitions." Accessed January 15, 2020. https://www.medicalnewstoday.com/articles/324437#types-of-bipolar-disorder

Link, Rachael. 2020. "8 Surprising Health Benefits of Cloves." Accessed April 9, 2020. https://www.healthline.com/nutrition/benefits-of-cloves

MacGill, Markus. 2019. "How does bipolar disorder affect memory?" Accessed February 4, 2020.
https://www.medicalnewstoday.com/articles/314328

Madhusoodanan, Jyoti. 2019. "Complications of Hypothyroidism." Accessed November 1, 2019.
https://www.healthline.com/health/hypothyroidism/complications#1

Mann, Andrea. 2016. "From fighting colon cancer to arthritis, 8 great benefits of curry." Accessed June 3, 2019.
http://home.bt.com/lifestyle/wellbeing/like-a-bit-of-spice-8-great-health-benefits-of-curry-11363994131863

Mariant, David. "Surviving Bipolar". Accessed February 14, 2013. http://www.survivingbipolar.com/green_suicide.htm#2

Martin, B. 2006. "Phases and Symptoms of Bipolar Disorder." Psych Central. Accessed January 14, 2012.
https://psychcentral.com/lib/phases-and-symptoms-of-bipolar-disorder/

Mayo Clinic, 2018. "Bipolar Disorder." Accessed January 2, 2019.

https://www.mayoclinic.org/diseases-conditions/bipolar-disorder/diagnosis-treatment/drc-20355961

Mayo Clinic. 2020. "Bipolar Disorder." Accessed February 7, 2020. https://www.mayoclinic.org/diseases-conditions/bipolar-disorder/symptoms-causes/syc-20355955

Mayo Clinic. 2020. "Bipolar Disorder." Accessed February 5, 2020. https://www.mayoclinic.org/diseases-conditions/bipolar-disorder/symptoms-causes/syc-20355955

Mayo Clinic. 2020. "Hyperthyroidism (overactive thyroid)." Accessed March 3, 2020. https://www.mayoclinic.org/diseases-conditions/hyperthyroidism/symptoms-causes/syc-20373659

Mayo Clinic, 2017. "Vitamin D". Accessed March 9, 2020. https://www.google.com/search?q=benefits+of+vitamin+d&rlz=1C1NCHA_enUS589US598&oq=benefits+of+vitamin+d&aqs=chrome..69i57j0l7.10678j0j7&sourceid=chrome&ie=UTF-8

McElroy, S. L. 2002. "Correlates of Overweight and Obesity in 644 Patients with Bipolar Disorder." Accessed September 2, 2012. https://pubmed.ncbi.nlm.nih.gov/11926719/

McIntosh, James. 2018. "What is serotonin and what does it do?" Accessed January 3, 2020. https://www.medicalnewstoday.com/articles/232248

McQuillan, Susan. 2019. "Is Bipolar Disorder Increasing Your Risk of Developing Heart Disease?" Accessed January 12, 2020. https://www.psycom.net/bipolar-disorder-and-heart-disease/

MEDTV, 2020. "Wellbutrin Side Effects." Accessed November 12, 2012. http://depression.emedtv.com/wellbutrin/wellbutrin-side-effects.html

Mert, Derya. 2013. "Perspectives on reasons of medication nonadherence in psychiatric patients." Accessed September 25, 2019. https://www.ncbi.nlm.nih.gov/pmc/articles/PMC4298301/

Mind for better mental health. 2020. "Psychiatric medication." Accessed April 10, 2020. https://www.mind.org.uk/information-support/drugs-and-treatments/medication/your-right-to-refuse-medication/

Monson, Kristi. 2007. “Risperdal Side Effects.” Accessed April 10, 2013. http://schizophrenia.emedtv.com/risperdal/risperdal-side-effects.html

Najafi-Vosough, Roya. 2016. “Recurrence in Patients with Bipolar Disorder and Its Risk Factors.” Accessed June 5, 2019. https://www.ncbi.nlm.nih.gov/pmc/articles/PMC5139952/

Narita, Kosuke. 2011. “Volume Reduction of Ventromedial Prefrontal Cortex in Bipolar II Patients with Rapid Cycling: A Voxel-Based Morphometric Study.” Accessed July 7, 2013. https://www.sciencedirect.com/science/article/abs/pii/S0278584610004616

National Institute of Mental Health. 2019. “Bipolar Disorder Statistics.” Accessed January 7, 2020. https://www.nimh.nih.gov/health/statistics/index.shtml

Natural Endocrine Solutions. 2018. “Fluoride, Bromide, Chloride and Thyroid Health.” Accessed January 3, 2020. https://www.naturalendocrinesolutions.com/articles/fluoride-bromide-chloride-and-thyroid-health/

Nauert, Rick. 2018. “Link Between Bipolar and Hypertension.” Accessed December 10, 2018. https://psychcentral.com/news/2010/06/14/link-between-bipolar-and-hypertension/14542.html

Newton, Phil. 2009. “What is Dopamine?” Accessed January 3, 2020. https://www.psychologytoday.com/us/blog/mouse-man/200904/what-is-dopamine

Propst, Stephen. 2019. “10 Ways to Repair Your Self Esteem.” Accessed January 3, 2020. https://www.bphope.com/strengthening-your-self-esteem/

Purse, Marcia. 2009. “Anxiety Medications: Bipolar Disorder Medications Library.” Accessed January 16, 2013. http://bipolar.about.com/od/sedatives/a/anxiety_medications.htm

Purse, Marcia. 2020. “What is a Manic Episode?” Accessed June 1, 2020. https://www.verywellmind.com/how-to-recognize-a-manic-or-hypomanic-episode-380316

Robertson, Ruairi. 2018. “13 Benefits of Taking Fish Oil.” Accessed April 3, 2019. https://www.healthline.com/nutrition/13-benefits-of-fish-oil

Rodriguez, Diana. 2012. “Bipolar Disorder: Regain Your Self-Esteem.” Accessed February 2, 2020. https://www.everydayhealth.com/hs/bipolar-depression/self-esteem-with-bipolar-disorder/

Ruiz, Miguel. 1997. "The Four Agreements." San Rafael: Amber-Allen Publishing. Accessed May 8, 2020.
https://www.miguelruiz.com/the-four-agreements

Sachs, Gary. 2008. "Are Men or Women More Likely to Develop Bipolar Disorder?" Accessed June 6, 2013.
http://abcnews.go.com/Health/BipolarRiskFactors/story?id=4356077

Sauer, Patrick. 2016. "Manic Spending Puts Bipolar Patients at Risk for Financial Woes." Accessed December 19, 2019.
https://www.health.com/condition/bipolar/manic-spending-puts-bipolar-patients-at-risk-for-financial-woes

Sheehan, Jan. 2008. "Coping With Bipolar Mood Swings." Accessed January 3, 2019.
https://www.everydayhealth.com/bipolar-disorder/bipolar-disorder-mood-swings.aspx

Smith, Melinda. 2019. "Depression Symptoms and Warning Signs." Accessed April 4, 2020.
https://www.helpguide.org/articles/depression/depression-symptoms-and-warning-signs.htm

Streit, Lizzie. 2018. "10 Health Benefits of Cardamom, Backed by Science." Accessed June 3, 2019.
https://www.healthline.com/nutrition/cardamom-benefits

Surks, Martin. 2019. "Lithium and the thyroid." Accessed December 3, 2019.
https://www.uptodate.com/contents/lithium-and-the-thyroid

Swartz, Holly. 2014. "Psychotherapy for Bipolar Disorder in Adults: A Review of the Evidence." Accessed December 5, 2019.
https://www.ncbi.nlm.nih.gov/pmc/articles/PMC4536930/

Tartakovsky, Margarita. 2020. "Bipolar Disorder Fact Sheet." Accessed April 4, 2020.
https://psychcentral.com/bipolar/bipolar-disorder-fact-sheet/

Testa, Megan. 2010. "Civil Commitment in the United States." Accessed January 12, 2020.
https://www.ncbi.nlm.nih.gov/pmc/articles/PMC3392176/

The Bledsoe Firm. 2017. "Marriage (or Deciding to Divorce) When Your Spouse Suffers from Bipolar Disorder." Accessed January 2, 2019.
https://www.fieldsdennis.com/wp-content/uploads/2018/03/Marriage-or-Deciding-to-Divorce-When-Your-Spouse-Suffers-from-Bipolar-Disorder.pdf

Thompson, Dennis. 2010. "Can Bipolar Lead to Diabetes?" Accessed November 12, 2012.
http://www.everydayhealth.com/bipolar-disorder/can-bipolar-disorder-lead-to-diabetes.aspx

University of Michigan General Research Center. 2005. "Evidence of Brain Chemistry Abnormalities in Bipolar Disorder." Accessed March 4, 2013. http://bipolar.about.com/cs/menu_science/a/press_umich0210.htm

University of Texas Health Science Center. 2017. "Area of brain linked to bipolar disorder pinpointed." Accessed June 6, 2019. https://www.sciencedaily.com/releases/2017/01/170124144000.htm

Vann, Madeline. 2017. "9 Most Common Triggers for Bipolar Mood Episodes." Accessed January 3, 2020. https://www.everydayhealth.com/bipolar-disorder-pictures/biggest-triggers-of-bipolar-mood-swings.aspx

Vann, Madeline. 2010. "Are People with Bipolar Disorder Dangerous?" Accessed March 5, 2013. http://www.everydayhealth.com/bipolar-disorder/are-people-with-bipolar-disorder-dangerous.aspx

WebMD, 2019. "Everyday Tips for Living With Bipolar Disorder." Accessed March 3, 2020. https://www.webmd.com/bipolar-disorder/guide/living-healthy-life-with-bipolar#1

WebMD. 2019. "Bipolar Disorder and Sleep Problems." Accessed January 7, 2020. https://www.webmd.com/bipolar-disorder/guide/bipolar-disorder-and-sleep-problems#1

WebMD. 2019. "Bipolar Disorder." Accessed March 3, 2020. https://www.webmd.com/bipolar-disorder/mental-health-bipolar-disorder#1

WebMD. 2019. "Causes of Bipolar Disorder." Accessed March 5, 2020. https://www.webmd.com/bipolar-disorder/guide/bipolar-disorder-causes#1

WebMD. 2019. "Depression in Bipolar Disorder: What You Can Do." Accessed March 10, 2020. https://www.webmd.com/bipolar-disorder/guide/depression-symptoms#1

WebMD, 2020. "Bipolar Episodes With Mixed Features." Accessed March 3, 2020. https://www.webmd.com/bipolar-disorder/guide/mixed-bipolar-disorder#1

WebMD, 2020. "Psychotherapy for Bipolar Disorder." Accessed March 6, 2020. https://www.webmd.com/bipolar-disorder/guide/psychotherapy-bipolar-disorder#1

WebMD. 2010. "The benefits of Vitamin C." Accessed March 2, 2020. https://www.webmd.com/diet/features/the-benefits-of-vitamin-c#1

WebMD. 2020. "Bipolar Disorder and Self-Injury." Accessed January 3, 2020. https://www.webmd.com/bipolar-disorder/guide/bipolar-disorder-self-injury#1

Woods, 2015. "Diabetes in Bipolar Disorder Takes Its Toll." Accessed January 7, 2020. https://www.psychiatrictimes.com/view/diabetes-bipolar-disorder-takes-its-toll

Young, A.H. 2013. "Physical health of patients with bipolar disorder." Accessed September 25, 2019. https://onlinelibrary.wiley.com/doi/pdf/10.1111/acps.12117

York, Susan. 2017. "Understanding Psychosis in Bipolar Disorder." Accessed January 3, 2020. https://www.healthline.com/health/bipolar-disorder/bipolar-psychosis

Zelman, Kathleen. 2010. "The benefits of Vitamin C." Accessed March 2, 2020. https://www.webmd.com/diet/features/the-benefits-of-vitamin-c#1